GHOSTHUNTING
COLORADO

AMERICA'S
HAUNTED ROAD TRIP

Titles in the America's Haunted Road Trip Series

Ghosthunting Colorado
Ghosthunting Florida
Ghosthunting Kentucky
Ghosthunting Illinois
Ghosthunting Maryland
Ghosthunting Michigan
Ghosthunting New Jersey
Ghosthunting New York City
Ghosthunting North Carolina
Ghosthunting Ohio
Ghosthunting Ohio: On the Road Again
Ghosthunting Oregon
Ghosthunting Pennsylvania
Ghosthunting San Antonio, Austin, and Texas Hill Country
Ghosthunting Southern California
Ghosthunting Southern New England
Ghosthunting Texas
Ghosthunting Virginia

Chicago Haunted Handbook
Cincinnati Haunted Handbook
Haunted Hoosier Trails
More Haunted Hoosier Trails
Nashville Haunted Handbook
Spooked in Seattle
Twin Cities Haunted Handbook

GHOSTHUNTING COLORADO

KAILYN LAMB

CLERISY PRESS

Ghosthunting Colorado
First edition, third printing 2022

COPYRIGHT © 2016 by Kailyn Lamb

For further information, contact the publisher:

Clerisy Press
An imprint of AdventureKEEN
306 Greenup St.
Covington, KY 41011
clerisypress.com

Cataloging-in-Publication Data is available from the Library of Congress.
ISBN-13: 978-1-57860-559-0 (pbk.); ISBN: 978-1-57860-560-6 (ebook)
ISBN 978-1-57860-609-2 (hardcover)

Distributed by Publishers Group West
Printed in the United States of America

Editor: Michael O. Varhola
Cover Design: Scott McGrew

Cover and interior photos by Kailyn Lamb with the following exceptions: page 31 Molly Brown House Museum; page 34 TrueshowIII/Wikimedia Commons/CC0 1.0 (creativecommons.org/publicdomain/zero/1.0); page 48, 55, 80, 101, 115, 117, 155, 181, and 185 Bryan Bonner/Rocky Mountain Paranormal Research Society; page 73 Kvng/Wikimedia Commons/CC BY-SA 3.0 (creativecommons.org/licenses/by-sa/3.0); page 97, 129, 134, and 165 Jeffrey Beall/Flickr/CC BY-SA 3.0; page 109 Matt Wright/Wikimedia Commons/CC BY-SA 2.5 (creativecommons.org/licenses/by-sa/2.5); page 120 Manitou Springs Chamber of Commerce; page 140 Robert Tadlock/ Wikimedia Commons/CC BY 2.0 (creativecommons.org/licenses/by/2.0); page 142: Michael Gäbler/Wikimedia Commons/CC BY 3.0; page 145 Ty Nigh/Wikimedia Commons/CC BY 2.0; page 148 Jerrye and Roy Klotz/ Wikimedia Commons/CC BY-SA 3.0; page 160 Daniel Case/Wikimedia Commons/CC BY-SA 3.0; page 170 Mark Kiryluk/Central City Opera House; page 175 Denver Public Library

TABLE OF CONTENTS

Acknowledgments   viii

Welcome to America's Haunted Road Trip   x

Introduction   1

Denver Area   9

1   Croke-Patterson Mansion   *Denver*   10

2   Cheesman Park and the Denver Botanic Gardens
        Denver   17

3   Molly Brown House Museum   *Denver*   27

4   Oxford Hotel   *Denver*   34

     "STRANGLER'S ROW"   38

5   Denver's Infamous Brothels   *Denver*   42

6   Brown Palace Hotel   *Denver*   48

7   Tivoli Student Union   *Denver*   54

Front Range   61

8   Buffalo Bill's Grave   *Golden*   62

9   Red Rocks Amphitheatre   *Morrison*   68

10   Hotel Boulderado   *Boulder*   73

      "BOULDER THEATER"   78

11   Stanley Hotel   *Estes Park*   80

East   88

12   Summit Springs Battlefield   *Otis*   89

13   Sand Creek Massacre   *Chivington*   94

South Central   100

14   Bloody Espinosa Brothers   *Various Locations*   101

15   Broadmoor   *Colorado Springs*   107

16   Cave of the Winds   *Manitou Springs*   114

17   Crawford Family   *Manitou Springs*   120

        "COLORADO'S COFFIN RACES"   124

18   Miramont Castle   *Manitou Springs*   128

19   Museum of Colorado Prisons   *Cañon City*   134

West   139

20   City of Durango   *Durango*   140

21   City of Breckenridge   *Breckenridge*   148

22   Hotel Colorado   *Glenwood Springs*   155

23   Hotel Jerome   *Aspen*   160

24   Redstone Castle   *Redstone*   165

25   Gilpin County   *Central City and Black Hawk*   170

Additional Haunted Sites   175

26   Capitol Hill Thug   *Denver*   176

27   Denver Public Library (Central Branch)   *Denver*   179

28   Lumber Baron Inn and Gardens   *Denver*   181

29   Macky Auditorium at the University of Colorado Boulder
       Boulder   185

30   Gold Camp Road   *Colorado Springs*   189

31   College Inn at the University of Colorado Boulder
       Boulder   192

32   Meeker Massacre   *Meeker*   193

33   Old Chapel   *Lamar*   197

34   Colorado Springs Pioneers Museum   *Colorado Springs*   199

35   McIntyre House   *Douglas County*   202

Colorado Haunted Road Trip Travel Guide   205

Visiting Haunted Sites   206

Ghostly Resources   217

Bibliography   218

About the Author   220

Acknowledgments

THIS WAS MY FIRST TIME EVER WRITING A BOOK, and like any great project, I learned that it takes a village to get things done. To the following I send my warmest thanks.

My first set of thanks goes to Michael O. Varhola, who decided I was a good candidate to write this book, and then constantly pushed me to get it done. I feel lucky every day to have been selected to be a part of the America's Haunted Road Trip series, and he was instrumental in making that happen.

The Rocky Mountain Paranormal Research Society has been ghosthunting in Colorado for nearly two decades, which made them a wealth of information when searching for locations that may (or may not be) truly haunted. My thanks to them for letting me join in on a ghost tour of Capitol Hill, because even after two years of living there I had no idea that I was living across the street from the supposed most haunted buildings in Denver. In particular, Bryan Bonner let me pick his brain about locations, but also about what it means to be a ghosthunter.

To finish a book, you must have someone to publish it. Thanks to the staff at Clerisy Press for making this book happen. In particular I would like to thank Tim W. Jackson and Liliane Opsomer, who worked with me.

To the friends and family who acted as the first readers (and makeshift editors), I appreciate all the help and time you were willing to give. My mother, Janelle Pedigo, gave feedback on every chapter, and is as much in the book as I am. To the friends and family who supported me by preordering the book on Amazon months before it was set to be published, you have my eternal gratitude.

To my parents, both biological and not, thank you for pushing me toward a career that I love. To William Ryan for teaching me the joy of writing simply for the love of it. To Nicole Lamb for showing me that cooking and sharing a glass of wine is an excellent way to de-stress, and to Jeff Lamb for always being the logical one. It doesn't sound like a compliment, but it means more to me than you will ever know.

Finally to William Fitzhugh for always being there to push me to get things finished, and for teaching me that hard work and dedication almost always pays off.

To anyone who I may have forgotten, I truly apologize and send my sincere thanks to you as well.

Welcome to America's Haunted Road Trip

By virtue of the fact that you are reading
THIS, there is a pretty good chance you believe in ghosts, or are
at least open to the idea that something referred to as such might
be real. If so, you are in pretty good company, as surveys over the
years tend to generally show that more than half of all Americans
believe in them and other supernatural phenomena. Some 61%
of participants in a September 2013 *Huffington Post* poll, in fact,
indicated that they "believe some people have experienced ghosts"
(those overall numbers skew up by as much as 8% and down by
as much as 16% based on factors that include gender, age, political
affiliation, race, education, and geographical region).

Paranormal phenomena you or those you know might have
experienced can vary widely, from the subtle to the profound and
the comforting to the disturbing. Many people not seeking supernatural experiences have felt the presence or touch of recently
departed loved ones, for example, or have even seen them, often
just once, as if in final farewell. Others have at various points, and
perhaps in places reputed to be haunted, experienced things like
disembodied footsteps, inexplicable cold spots, or sounds with no
discernible source, such as someone calling their name.

Those who are psychically sensitive, are exposed to extremely
haunted sites, or actively engage in paranormal investigations of
various sorts—including what have been widely referred to for
some years now as ghosthunts—might experience any number

of other things as well. These can include anomalies not audible to the unaided ear or visible to the naked eye that are captured in recordings or photographs, such as electronic voice phenomena (EVP) in the former and orbs, mists, or even coveted "full-frontal apparitions" in the latter.

Our intent with the America's Haunted Road Trip series is to provide readers with resources they can use to personally discover and explore publicly accessible places that might be occupied by ghosts or the sites of other paranormal activity. We are not in the business of trying to prove that any particular place is or is not haunted; every single one of the places that appears in *Ghosthunting Colorado* certainly could be, and we believe that a number of them definitely are. The purpose of this volume and the others in the series is, rather, to tell everyone from the casual historical traveler to the hard-core ghosthunter about places of potential interest and to provide actionable, concrete information about how to visit those places.

As noted, all of the places covered in this book and the other volumes of the America's Haunted Road Trip series are, to a lesser or greater extent, publicly accessible; there is simply no point in creating a travel guide to places people cannot easily visit. Places we cover in our guidebooks therefore include appropriate bridges; churches and other places of worship; cemeteries and graveyards; colleges and universities; government buildings; historic sites; hotels; museums; neighborhoods/districts of towns or cities; parks; restaurants and bars; roads and highways; railroads; shopping areas and malls; sports stadiums; and theaters.

Places we do not cover in our guidebooks or encourage people to visit generally include elementary, middle, or high schools; hospitals; assisted-living facilities; private homes and residential apartment buildings; private property; or prohibited areas like abandoned mental institutions or condemned buildings. It also bears mentioning that all potentially haunted places, their intersection with the otherworld notwithstanding, are still subject to all the hazards of the real world. So, show due respect to other good people and watch out for bad ones, do not violate local laws, be prepared for environmental hazards, and, in keeping with the mantra of urban exploration, "take nothing but photographs; leave nothing but footprints."

Beyond that, we hope this book and the others in the series will be useful to you and that you have an enjoyable, informative, and fulfilling journey on your own haunted road trip.

Michael O. Varhola
Editor, America's Haunted Road Trip

Introduction

"Jack stood in the dining room just outside the batwing doors leading into the Colorado Lounge, his head cocked, listening. He was smiling faintly. Around him, he could hear the Overlook Hotel coming to life."

— Stephen King, *The Shining*

FOR 20 YEARS OF MY LIFE I have lived in Denver or in the metropolitan area surrounding it. Denver is an ideal city. It has all of the excitement that city life brings but is also a short and easy drive away from the beauty of the mountains. It is the Rocky Mountain State, forged on the blood and sweat of miners, and in some places unfortunately scarred by the angry battles between the American Indian tribes who called these lands home and the settlers who were trying to make it theirs.

Probably the most surprising thing I found as I dove head-first into the supposed haunted areas of Colorado is how much their stories were rooted in history. Some places were actually able to trace their ghostly stories to real events that happened there. This feeling was mirrored by Bryan Bonner, co-founder of the Rocky Mountain Paranormal Research Society. Bonner and the rest of the RMPRS make it their mission to search for ghosts using science and logic and, for them, the first step is almost always research.

Research means being able to separate urban legends from what actually happened. Knowing the background of a location can help a researcher understand why any sort of paranormal activity might be happening there. Bonner used an old inn in Evergreen, Colorado, as an example. The ghost story was that the original owner's son had died in the building as a child of a lung condition and has been running up and down the halls bouncing a ball as a spirit since then. After doing research at the Evergreen Library for a couple of years, they found an obituary from 1922 saying that the son died of pneumonia at the house.

"It doesn't prove that it's a ghost, but it's a huge piece of a puzzle to at least say, well, some of these stories we're hearing are true. The original owner's son did die of a lung condition," Bonner said. The inn, which is now privately owned and will not let RMPRS come in for any more investigations, provides a good example of the importance of visiting sites multiple times if possible. While not every location will allow someone to investigate as many times as they might like, the more you visit, the more information you can collect.

Before I ever knew about ghosthunting, I lived in Denver and interacted with many of these locations on a regular basis. Tivoli on the Auraria college campus was where I spent a large amount of time while working on Metropolitan State University of Denver's student newspaper. Spending late nights in a dark brewery turned student union is enough to raise the hair on anyone's neck. One of the strangest coincidences, however, was that I lived in an apartment directly across the street from the Croke-Patterson Mansion. For the first year I lived there, I was completely ignorant that the building across the street from me had a reputation for being one of the most haunted buildings in Denver. Despite not knowing, I definitely felt that the building had a presence, and I would often wonder what the inside of the massive red sandstone structure looked like. Once I began writing, I was quickly hooked on the mansion's story, and it became hard to let it go.

Croke-Patterson Mansion is far from being the only haunted hotel in Colorado; in fact, as many know, it is not even considered to be the most haunted one. That honor goes to the Stanley Hotel in Estes Park. I doubt that I have to tell many paranormal enthusiasts, but the Stanley is the location that inspired Stephen King's *The Shining*. That book, which was King's third novel, is only one of his works that is located in Colorado. While King typically writes about his home state of Maine, he occasionally branches out to the Centennial State. The Stanley is one of the few locations I know of that fully embraces its haunted reputation, and even profits from it.

While all of the locations in this book are worth the visit, I have to say I have a personal favorite—yet another location I interacted with before knowing it was haunted. It is an unwritten rule that all true Coloradans must see a concert at Red Rocks Amphitheatre. But I try to get out there whenever I have the time, and not just for concerts. I never felt any malicious spirits, but the area certainly has magic of a different kind, and I never feel more at peace than when I am at Red Rocks surrounded by the mountains. The same can be said of many of the mountainous locations in this book, and the Rockies are simply beautiful to behold. Their giant presence in Colorado Springs inspired Katharine Lee Bates to write the poem "Pikes Peak," more commonly known today as "America the Beautiful," and the "purple mountain majesties" that she writes about stretch across the entire state.

As a local Coloradan, I had no idea just how surrounded by ghost stories I was and, despite having written a book on the subject, I still consider myself to be a novice ghosthunter. There are many aspects to consider beyond researching a location and determining how much of its story is legend versus history. This is where the RMPRS, whose members have been investigating paranormal stories across the state of Colorado since 1999, comes in. In the times that I met with Bonner, I noticed something very important about his group's philosophy: the RMPRS are not ghosthunters. They have created the term Paranormal Claim Investigators for themselves to better explain what they do. That means that instead of going to locations anticipating finding ghosts, the group tries to look at every possible scientific or logical explanation before looking to otherworldly explanations. Bonner says they use the rule of Ockham's Razor, the scientific idea that, given all explanations, the simplest is usually the most accurate. Even if the simplest explanations fall through, they do not jump to ghostly conclusions and will simply state that they could not find any reason for the particular activity.

"We investigate the claims; we don't go in to find the ghost," Bonner said. "We go 'OK, what supposedly has happened here?' and then we break each one of the claims down individually." The group go out of their way to decipher urban legends to separate those from the true history of a location and investigate every possible explanation for the strange occurrences their clients bring to them.

Depending on the location, the RMPRS may use any of several branches of science to look at what could be causing paranormal activity. The group has consulted physicists, geologists, psychologists, and many other experts depending on the question at hand. While the members of RMPRS have started to use some of these skills themselves in their investigations, Bonner said that their most important tool is critical thinking.

"All this stuff doesn't mean anything if you're not applying it right," Bonner said. He also mentioned that on occasion, aside from scientific experts, the group has been known to consult magicians for their ability to think outside the box.

I learned a number of things about visiting haunted locations from my conversations with Bonner. First and foremost is to keep an open mind, which prevents you from going into an investigation either thinking the location is not haunted at all or "knowing" it is haunted. This helps prevent what Bonner likes to call "confirmation bias," where a team goes in based on previously collected evidence and automatically decides a location is haunted. Bonner said that an example of confirmation bias is ghosthunters going to a location and recording electronic voice phenomena (EVP) sessions in which they begin asking questions of any ghosts that might be present. He explained that at that point, an investigator is no longer questioning whether there is something paranormal present.

"If you're talking to the ghost already, psychologically you've just set yourself up to 'Yes, there's a ghost here, and I'm going to talk to it,' " he said. For this reason, among others, Bonner and his team have a process of selecting which locations to actually investigate. From there they do their research on the history of the site, including interviewing people about their experiences.

Once they have a thorough background on the location—something they will sometimes spend months or even years on—they decide what equipment to bring.

"There are a lot of things claiming to be ghost meters, sensors, or cameras. It's a marketing tool," Bonner said. He added that it is important to have a good knowledge of how the equipment works, as none of it was originally made for ghosthunting or to properly evaluate the findings and their meaning. Both Bonner and another member of the RMPRS team, Matthew Baxter, have become certified in different kinds of equipment, from cameras, computers, and video recorders, to some more sophisticated devices such as Electromagnetic Field (EMF) readers. This is a particular favorite of Bonner's to explain, because it is one of the pieces of equipment that television ghosthunters misuse the most. There are two kinds of readers: one finds man-made electronic items, such as wiring and televisions, and the other reads naturally occurring electronic fields.

"The only problem is it detects you, changes in the ionosphere, a thunderstorm 10 or 20 miles away. There are a lot of things that it's not really good to use unless you're really trained in it," Bonner said. This means that when ghosthunters on television are carrying around EMF readers that are meant to find natural electric waves, the things they detect are not necessarily ghosts. The reader is more likely picking up the waves of the person holding the device rather than any paranormal beings.

This small example is one reason why both Bonner and Baxter have made sure to learn more about the equipment they use regularly in their investigations. Bonner also said that sometimes they have been able to resolve cases just by moving electronics to different areas so that they are not affecting people. They have a full list of other equipment that they bring depending on what the investigation requires. One item is an iPhone, or any other Apple product, for its 3-D accelerometer, which Bonner said can be used as an incredibly effective seismometer in conjunction with software for creating graphs.

Another thing to remember is not to buy into all the hype and practices of television ghosthunters. Most of what they do is for ratings. This is another thing the RMPRS can testify to firsthand, having been asked to participate in ghosthunting shows before. However, RMPRS sticks to its guns (and its science) and refuses to join in on the trend.

"When we do an investigation, it's boring," Baxter said of his group's ghosthunting technique. "We go in, we set up all our equipment, and then we shut up. You see, if we make noise, it contaminates our own evidence, and then it's worthless."

As far as collecting evidence goes, RMPRS also tries to keep the site of an investigation in the exact condition it was in when the activity was reported. As an example of what not to do, Bonner cited television ghosthunters always turning off the lights (unless the person actually saw the ghost in the dark). The science behind ghosthunting is also key. One of the more popular claims of many television investigators is that ghosts leave cold spots. Bonner, however, disagrees and uses basic physics to explain why.

"They say that the reason that a cold spot happens is because when a ghost tries to manifest, tries to move something, does something, it extracts energy from the air to do whatever it is and that creates a cold spot," he said. "This is a really simple physics question. I've asked a lot of people, and the kids get it all the time; the adults, no: anytime there's an exchange of energy the byproduct is heat. If anything, we should be looking for hot spots."

Ghosthunting can have a very serious side as well. One of Bonner's biggest concerns is ghosthunting cases where people are so desperate to believe that their home is haunted that they are causing themselves psychological harm. Bonner said that, sadly, this is something most ghosthunters ignore. He added that most of the time RMPRS is not the first team the clients have called and, if that is the case, the team ends up doing damage control. Because many of the more popular ghosthunting groups are on TV—or are copying what they see on TV— they are doing things for the producers and the ratings, not necessarily for the claims they are investigating. He also mentioned cases where people have started causing physical harm to themselves or others.

These are the sorts of cases where it is probably best not to be involved. In researching a location before visiting, you may find that many of the supposedly haunted locations found on the Internet are not on public property. While some property owners may not have a problem with people looking around, there are also locations where the owners have made it quite clear they do not want people investigating any paranormal activity. In either case it is smart to check it out first, and always ask permission.

The world is full of interesting history and, with it, an occasional ghost story. With the right tools and a little bit of critical thinking, you might just strike paranormal gold. Even though the RMPRS founders are hesitant to say whether their findings have ever led to ghosts, Baxter remains somewhat positive.

"You can't prove a negative, so we can't say any place isn't haunted," Baxter said.

Please enjoy this book of haunted locations in Colorado. I hope you find the history of the state as fascinating as I do. Whether or not you find ghosts is up for debate, but I do think you will find magic of a different kind in the mountains.

Kailyn Lamb
New York, New York
April 2016

Denver Area

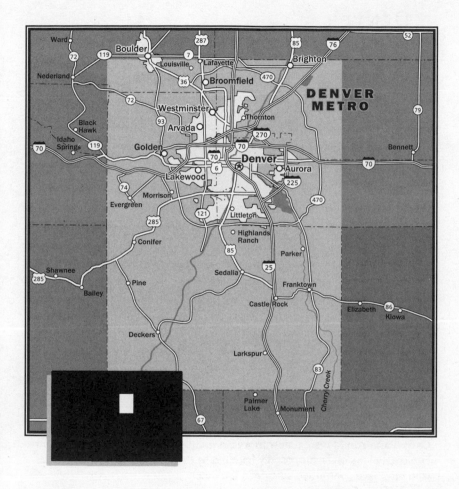

Denver Area

Croke-Patterson Mansion

Cheesman Park and the Denver
  Botanic Gardens

Molly Brown House Museum

Oxford Hotel

Denver's Infamous Brothels

Brown Palace Hotel

Tivoli Student Union

CHAPTER 1

Croke-Patterson Mansion
DENVER

On the corner of 11th Avenue and Pennsylvania Street stands the monstrous Croke-Patterson Mansion, now more commonly known as the Patterson Inn. The large mansion is supposedly haunted by the wife of a previous owner, who may have committed suicide in the house.

CROKE-PATTERSON MANSION notoriously fits in with Capitol Hill's most famous homes, but the house has also taken on a life of its own. Standing on the corner of 11th Avenue and Pennsylvania Street, the house fills three lots and is made of beautiful red stones most likely taken from what is now the Garden of the Gods park near Manitou Springs, Colorado. Its looks alone are enough to make passersby stare in wonder, but it is the mansion's history as one of the most haunted houses in Colorado that makes it really amazing. With a dance card of séances, deaths, suicide, an alleged satanic carriage-house keeper, and human-shaped apparitions, it is clear why the looming red sandstone structure has an aura about it. Although many of the stories tied to the house have little to no root in truth, the house does have a colorful history that makes its red coloring very fitting.

Thomas B. Croke was a teacher from Wisconsin who came to Denver and made his fortune as a businessman. After purchasing a lot around 1890, Croke commissioned architect Isaac Hodgson Jr. to build the 14,000-square-foot mansion, which he completed in 1891. Hodgson had already built several other houses in the area and, much like his other designs, this mansion's architecture was inspired by that of French châteaus. According to the current owner, architect Brian Higgins, it is the last remaining châteauesque house in Denver.

From the beginning, Croke-Patterson Mansion had a reputation. A basic Internet search on the house brings up several websites that tell a "legendary" tale of how Croke was not able to spend even one day in his new home because something felt wrong about it. Real estate records reveal, however, that Croke lived in the house for six months, and the real culprit for his vacating the mansion was more likely the crash of the silver market. In addition, Croke's wife passed away before the house's completion, leaving him a widower as well as a single parent. Croke's parents also joined him living in the house, but his mother died shortly after moving in.

Records and letters show that Croke later traded the house for land that was owned by Thomas Patterson, perhaps the house's most well-known owner. Patterson was a US Senator for the state of Colorado for one term, from 1901 to 1907. He

previously had served in the United States House of Representa-
tives in Colorado's 1st district when the territory first became a
state, serving from 1877 to 1879. Patterson was also the owner of
the *Rocky Mountain News*, Colorado's first newspaper. He lived
in the house with his wife, Katherine, and daughters, Mary and
Margaret. Patterson also had a son, James, who had committed
suicide in California before the family moved into the house.

Mary died of chronic illness in 1894 and after the death of
his wife in 1902, Patterson deeded the house to his daughter
Margaret and her husband, Richard C. Campbell (the house is
sometimes called the Croke-Patterson-Campbell house). Patterson
lived in the house a total of 23 years, until his death in July of
1916. The Campbells continued to live in the mansion until
1924, the longest any single family ever did.

The Campbells sold the house to the Louise Realty Company.
Before becoming home to another family, the mansion changed
hands and uses several times. However, the next family to live
in the Croke-Patterson Mansion is frequently skipped over in
online accounts of its history.

Dr. Archer Sudan purchased and moved into the house in
1947. Sudan was president of the Colorado Medical Association
and moved his practice from the mountains to Denver. His wife,
Tulleen, who was also a nurse, accompanied him. They also had
a son, Archer Jr., who did not live with them in the mansion,
as he was old enough to live on his own at the time. Although
Tulleen was said to be happy and social, she committed suicide
in the house in 1950 using cyanogas, a powerful pesticide, in
one of the bathrooms. It was rumored that the reason behind
her suicide was that she had a miscarriage.

What is most surprising about these residents being
excluded from most written histories of the house is that it is
the supposed ghost of Tulleen Sudan that permeates most of
the tales. A woman who lost her baby looking longingly out the

third-floor window, the sounds of a crying baby when no one is in the house, and the supposed burial of a baby in the basement are among the accounts related to her. There is also a rumor that the baby was murdered. Tulleen, however, was 47 when she died, past the age of healthy childbearing, and there is no record of a child being born in the house. Some people who have entered the house even claim that they begin to feel as if they cannot breathe when walking up the stairs to the third floor. Cyanogas creates cyanide when combined with moisture, effectively suffocating anyone close enough to be exposed to the gas. Supposedly, Tulleen used a bathtub full of water, creating the cyanide to kill herself. Dr. Sudan continued to live in the house after Tulleen's death until 1958. After he and his second wife moved out of the house, Archer Jr. moved into the mansion, serving as landlord for the separate apartments his father had created upon moving in. Records show it was sold in October 1972.

Many of the stories of apparitions point to Tulleen's spirit having never left the house after her death. But there is more to the story of the mansion. History major Mary Rae, who along with her husband became the next owner in April 1973, helped save it from demolition and later helped make it a historic landmark (Colorado's Landmark Preservation Commission Ordinance 457, July 1973).

Rae made many improvements to the deteriorating building, including cleaning out the basement, which she claims to have cleared of fetuses, brains, fingers, and other body parts in jars that were presumably collected by Archer Jr., who was also a doctor. Rae also continued to keep the apartment structure that the Sudans used when residing in the building but never lived in the house herself. Several of her tenants would leave in the middle of the night without paying, too scared to stay in the building. Many claimed to hear babies crying on the third floor, even though there were none living in the building at the time, and there was no one living in the room the sounds were reportedly coming from, which was used for storage. The mansion had quickly become a financial sinkhole, so Rae sold it in 1976.

In the late '70s, the building was renovated to become an office space. Construction workers would leave for the night, only to come back the next day and find all their previous day's work undone. Suspecting that people, and not ghosts, were behind it, workers put a fence around the building, and when that did not work they brought in a guard, who quit after one night. Next, guard dogs were brought in to protect the work site. There are multiple accounts of what happened next, but they all agree on one thing: one of the dogs jumped from a tower window in the building on the first night and died of his injuries within several days. According to other versions of the story, another one was also mortally injured on the second night. The other guard dog was found in the basement in a catatonic state, in which he remained for the rest of his life.

Despite these setbacks, the office space was eventually completed, but the hauntings did not stop, and employees would hear typewriters and other office supplies being used when there was no one around. Many tied this to Thomas Patterson, saying that some scandal or story had not made it into the paper, so a departed Patterson was going to do it himself.

One person, who owned the building in 1998, claims to have seen ghosts and witnessed household items move on their own. One resident of the building in 2004 claims to have seen apparitions of a maid who would go up and down the stairs, with only her upper body and torso visible and her legs seeming to dissipate. There is also a story of the ghost of Katherine Patterson helping a pregnant resident roll over.

Rocky Mountain Paranormal Research Society (RMPRS) has worked with the current and previous owners of the building, such as Dr. Douglas Ikeler and his wife, Melodee. Bryan

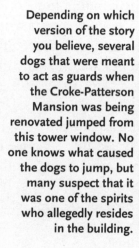

Depending on which version of the story you believe, several dogs that were meant to act as guards when the Croke-Patterson Mansion was being renovated jumped from this tower window. No one knows what caused the dogs to jump, but many suspect that it was one of the spirits who allegedly resides in the building.

Bonner of RMPRS says that he heard the story of the pregnant woman firsthand from Melodee, who lived in the mansion with her husband for 10 years. Bonner added that, including the owners he has personally worked with, anyone who has been in contact with the mansion for long periods of time seems to start to "lose it." He used Tulleen Sudan as a prime example.

RMPRS also did a radio show out of the mansion during one of the periods it was vacant. Its members decided they were going to stay the night there for the show. One of the sound engineers stayed in the basement. According to Bonner, he came back upstairs immediately, saying there was a man standing in the corner. They searched the mansion but could not find a man. Bonner added, however, that it was the same corner of the basement where the catatonic dog was found, and it was the same corner that the Ikelers' daughters had previously claimed to have seen a man standing by their toys.

The house remained vacant for a while before its most current owner, Brian Higgins, and his business partner at the time, Travis McAfoos, purchased the building in hopes of turning it into a bed-and-breakfast. According to Bonner, Higgins at first planned to completely renovate the building to its original historic state, but changed his mind entirely after staying in the mansion. Higgins decided to film the renovations on the building, documenting his own "hauntings" and mishaps that occurred while the work was in progress. Higgins' documentary, which he directed, edited, and titled *The Castle Project,* begs the question as to whether he believes in the haunts that reside in his bed-and-breakfast. Higgins, who stayed in the house for several days during the renovation, filmed a bat flying around the building at night and caught footage of an apparition of a maid in the large mirror on the main floor of the house. He also recorded audio of disembodied voices. Contractors working on the renovation also reported seeing shadows and apparitions, as well as feeling cold spots, smelling putrid odors, and hearing noises such as music, babies crying, and other voices. A fire, which Higgins claims started the same night as the Waldo Canyon fires near Colorado Springs at that time, caused several setbacks in renovation.

After an 18-month renovation, the mansion was reopened in August 2012 as the Patterson Bed and Breakfast. Since then, it has landed on CBS's top 10 bed-and-breakfasts list, in July 2014. With nine themed rooms and accommodations such as large flat-screen TVs, Higgins has worked hard to erase the stigma surrounding the Croke-Patterson Mansion. He renovated it for the modern world but kept some of the historical Victorian-era design, such as the mansion's famed stained-glass windows. For the cost of spending a night there, paranormal enthusiasts can decide for themselves whether the mansion is still haunted.

CHAPTER 2

Cheesman Park and the Denver Botanic Gardens

DENVER

The Denver Botanic Gardens are now on top of where the Catholic section of Denver's cemetery used to be. Supposedly one of the classrooms in the atrium building (pictured) is haunted.

THE FIELDS OF GREEN GRASS and looping sidewalks between Eighth and 13th Avenues that make up Cheesman Park look like any other city recreational area. There are trees, joggers, and groups playing volleyball or Ultimate Frisbee. It is also, however, the former location of a graveyard and body dump site.

The land on which Cheesman Park currently resides was used by the Arapahoe tribe that inhabited parts of Colorado before it became a territory. In 1858, General William Larimer founded the city of Denver, setting aside 160 acres for a cemetery. Because the land was originally sacred burial grounds for the Arapahoe tribe, Denver had to follow very specific rules when using the land as a cemetery. American Indians were buried there at the typical 6 feet underground and, because new burials were not allowed to disturb the previous ones, they were placed only 3 feet under. This land would later be split among Cheesman Park, Congress Park, and the Denver Botanic Gardens. Larimer designated a corner of the cemetery for Denver's up-and-coming wealthy upper class, while the opposite corner was for criminals and the poor. The middle class was set in the middle.

The first recorded burial in the newly named Mount Prospect Cemetery was a man who died from a lung infection. The second burial was much more interesting. John Stoefel, having been tried and convicted by the people's court for the murder of his brother-in-law, was hanged from a tree and buried in the cemetery. Despite being a new territory with only a few residents, nearly 1,000 people came to witness Stoefel's hanging, which is listed as the first official execution in Colorado. He was buried in April of 1859 in the same grave as his victim, Thomas Beincroff.

More and more, the poor section of the cemetery was filled with outlaws and criminals. When professional gambler Jack O'Neal was shot outside a saloon in Denver, he was buried in Mount Prospect in March 1860, and the *Rocky Mountain News* printed a story in which it gave the cemetery the nickname "Jack O'Neal's Ranch."

Mount Prospect never became the beautiful garden cemetery Larimer had envisioned. Denver's wealthy buried their dead in other locations, leaving the area to the diseased, the outlaws, and the poor. After Larimer left Denver in the late 1860s, the cemetery was taken over by aspiring undertaker John Walley. Walley was a cabinetmaker, which may explain why the land and graves quickly went into disrepair under his watch. Although he supervised many of the burials, he allegedly made poor caskets with as little lumber as possible. Gravestones began to topple, and many were vandalized. Cattle reportedly grazed the grass of the cemetery and homesteaders lived off of its land.

Religious groups began sectioning off certain parts of the cemetery for their dead. Catholics purchased 40 acres of land from Walley in August of 1865, located by modern-day Eighth to 11th Avenues on one end and from High to Race Streets on the other, and, after christening the property, named it Mount Calvary. East of this cemetery from York to Josephine Streets and Ninth to 11th Avenues was the Hebrew Cemetery, which was fenced off, on land purchased from Walley by Jews in August 1866. This same year, reports say, a total of 626 people were buried in Mount Prospect, Mount Calvary, and the Hebrew Cemetery.

But many argued that Walley had no claim to the land. In response to the city of Denver's reaching out to Washington to settle disputes on who truly owned the cemetery land, the US government reclaimed the area and declared it federal property in March 1870. The government in turn resold 160 acres to the city of Denver for $200 after the city requested it for burial purposes. In May 1872, Congress specified that the land must always be used for burials, and the ground was renamed Denver City Cemetery.

Water was not available for irrigation in this area until 1888, and because of this, landscaping in the cemetery was difficult. Mount Calvary and the Hebrew Cemetery are often cited as the more well-kept areas of the burial ground, while the rest remained hardly touched. The cemetery also started to be plagued by stories of grave robbing, body snatching by medical students, and corrupt undertakers removing old bodies to put in new ones. Supposedly, these evicted corpses would be found in the streets surrounding the graveyard. Softer clay beneath the graves also created problems, as it caused some of the coffins to shift positions and the ground above them to settle.

With the establishment of the private Riverside Cemetery in 1876 and Fairmount Cemetery in 1890, many graves were removed from Denver City Cemetery in favor of the two new locations. As the public cemetery became increasingly ignored, these competitors called for its closing, and it became clear that the burial ground was on its last leg. In January 1890, Congress finally agreed to Denver's request to make the cemetery a park. As a sign of thanks for this, it was originally named Congress Park. But first, to create a proper park, the bodies and graves needed to be moved.

It is the story of how the bodies were removed from what would eventually become Cheesman Park that causes the spine-tingling stories of a haunted city park. The city gave families of the dead 90 days to remove the bodies. Not all of the bodies were claimed, however, and some bodies were not actually in their specified locations due to poor record keeping; cemetery records showed nearly 5,000 bodies remained, but there may have been thousands more. In addition, according to the Rocky Mountain Paranormal Research Society, because Denver was a "pass through" city for a long period of time, hundreds of the bodies no longer had families to claim them.

Enter Edward P. McGovern, whom the city hired to remove the rest of the graveyard's occupants for $1.90 per casket. Often McGovern found bones scattered and not in once piece, bodies not where they were supposed to be, and more than one occupant in some graves. He also found evidence that solidified the stories of grave robberies. Also, because the bodies were buried in shallow graves, the acidic soil ate through both the caskets and flesh very quickly, leaving just skeletons in the burial sites.

It is how McGovern started moving the bodies, using smaller child-size caskets and often cutting bodies into pieces to fit, that got him in trouble. Sometimes bodies were split between multiple caskets; even more frequently body parts were simply left behind, and there are rumors that parts from more than one body were placed in some caskets. While some claim that McGovern did this for the money, there is also the story that, due to a large mining accident in Utah, Denver had a shortage of adult caskets, as they had sent a large number of those available to the accident. Other rumors that destroyed McGovern's reputation claimed that he began stripping corpses of their valuables. Because of the haste in which the job was being done, onlookers could see the body parts haphazardly thrown about and were even able to take "souvenirs" themselves. Once *The Denver Republican* caught wind of the story, the newspaper ran it with the criminalizing headline "The Work of Ghouls" in March 1893. Although the scandal got McGovern dismissed from the job, he continued to thrive in his position as city coroner until his death, and his mortuary continued as well in the wake of the scandal. Beyond all that, the city never hired a replacement undertaker to finish the job.

Interestingly enough, McGovern became falsely associated with Croke-Patterson Mansion (page 10). The satanic undertaker that supposedly lived in the carriage house of the mansion is often thought to be McGovern, most likely because of his work in Cheesman Park, but this spirit is most often called "Willie." In addition to the holding of satanic rituals, the wild stories also say there was a young boy murdered and later hanged from a tree in the yard of the mansion. People claim that the dead bodies from Cheesman were not enough for the carriage house occupant and that he eventually began kidnapping people off the street. The metal beam on the upper floor of the carriage house was supposedly where he would hang bodies after he killed them in his

This stage area in Cheesman Park was once used for performances of Broadway show tunes and other theater pieces. It's rumored that in some areas of the park, patches of grass grow greener because they mark the site of a grave.

rituals. There is also a now-closed tunnel that he supposedly used to transport bodies from the main house to the carriage house. There are, however, no records that anyone lived in the carriage house, or that it had other uses outside of such a building's normal functions. In fact, real estate records also show that McGovern lived in an entirely different house on Pennsylvania Street.

Despite the number of bodies removed from Cheesman Park by McGovern and the families of the dead, it is estimated that 2,000–3,000 remain there. Close observers of the park may note that parts of the grass have rectangular plots that are lower than others and that in the spring some plots, also rectangular in shape, become green faster than others. Park goers also report cold spots throughout the park or the feeling of hands grabbing their ankles as they walk through the grass. Some also claim to have seen ghostly limbs or other body parts lying around, and others still have reported seeing ghostly figures looking for their own remains—the most horrifying of which are missing their heads.

This ties in with widespread ghostly lore that the spirits of the dead cannot properly rest if their bodies are not intact or in one piece. Supposedly, under the right type of moonlight, visitors can also see the ghostly shapes of old gravestones in the park.

Because of the type of clay soil Colorado has in this area, much of which is found in Cheesman Park, caskets and skeletons have been known to move or shift positions. On a haunted tour with the Rocky Mountain Paranormal Research Society, Matthew Baxter and Bryan Bonner will paint a picture typical of scary movies in which a ghostly hand reaches through the soil to grab someone's ankle. They go on to say that, due to the shifting clay, bones can really shift to the surface of the park.

Because of a lack of funds, the park initially remained fenced off and untamed from 1894 to 1898. In the early 1900s the park did open but lacked a lot of architect Reinhard Schuetze's original designs, such as a pavilion. Mayor Robert Speer offered anyone who would donate the funds to build the pavilion the right to name the park. The wife and daughter of recently deceased Walter Cheesman donated $100,000, giving the place its current name. Construction of the pavilion started in 1908, and it still stands today. Of the 320 acres originally used for Mount Prospect, only 81 were used for Cheesman Park; the rest were allocated for the new Congress Park and the Denver Botanic Gardens.

On occasion, when work is being done in Cheesman Park, such as in 2010 when the city was digging a new irrigation system, skeletal remains are found and then reburied in a different location by the municipality.

DENVER BOTANIC GARDENS AND THE SURROUNDING AREA

IN 1892, local Catholics moved their burial grounds from the York Street area of Mount Calvary to Mount Olivet Cemetery, although interments continued in the original location until 1908. It was finally sealed off in 1910. Twenty acres of the Catholic cemetery were sold to a real estate developer to create Morgan's Addition in 1887. Development of the land began in 1903 and was quickly used for homes for the wealthy. The few houses that remain surround the Cheesman Park area and sit next to the land that became the Denver Botanic Gardens.

In 1950, Denver had convinced the Catholic archdiocese to deed the remaining property of Mount Calvary back to the city. After an excavation of the remaining bodies, two-thirds of which were infants, the land was riddled with holes. Through much of the decade it remained this way, unlandscaped and fenced off. Meanwhile, the City Park Botanic Gardens was not doing as well as the city had hoped. City Park was a more active area, which caused difficulty with the rose gardens. Due to little policing, the area was also frequently vandalized.

Originally, in 1953, the gardens were to be housed in a 100-acre plot of land on the eastern edge of City Park, near the already-established Denver Museum of Natural History and the Denver Zoo off of Colorado Boulevard. The city went so far as to start planting rose gardens, as well as a lilac lane that was placed between the zoo and the museum.

In 1958, it was decided that some of the gardens would be moved to the Mount Calvary grounds, the idea being to protect the plants from the damage happening at City Park. Within a few years, however, the entirety of the gardens was moved to the York Street location. After receiving a grant in 1963 to build what is now the gardens' centerpiece, Boettcher Conservatory, the location was formally dedicated in 1966.

Morgan's Addition, mentioned earlier, became an important part of the life of the gardens. One house in particular, 909 York St., was donated by residents from Morgan's Addition. The house was originally owned by none other than Margaret Patterson

Campbell and her husband, Richard, of Croke-Patterson Mansion fame. In April 1959, the house opened as part of Denver Botanic Gardens, and it is used today as administrative offices.

In Kevin Pharris's book *The Haunted Heart of Denver,* he recounts his time as a volunteer at Denver Botanic Gardens and, specifically, his encounters with this house. Before writing the book, Pharris gave historical tours of Denver and eventually transitioned to giving haunted tours, and the botanic gardens asked him to write a haunted tour for them. While he did hear stories about dark clouds floating around the classroom areas in the gardens, the Campbells' house at Ninth and York seemed to hold more. This house had secret passages, as did many old houses, and one secret door led to a small room with a narrow, steep staircase leading to a bedroom. According to Pharris, the stairs lift to reveal another secret passage, but no one who works in the house is willing to do this, as it supposedly awakens and angers the ghosts who reside there. Workers report that if the passage under the stairs is opened, the house becomes plagued by strange sounds and objects are moved when no one has been there. This continues for several weeks, losing strength and frequency as time passes, until the ghosts again resume "sleeping."

Residents of Morgan's Addition strongly influenced the future of Denver Botanic Gardens. Some were on the board for the gardens, while others engaged with the city in secret meetings dealing with the residentially disliked, yet popular, concerts for which the gardens had become known. Summer concert series are still held there today.

Although many of the mansions did not survive and were demolished, some of the stories of homes in the surrounding Cheesman Park area carry stories of ghosts that live to this day. One such house on 13th Avenue was rented by Broadway and Hollywood composer Russell Hunter in 1968. He claims that in the spring of 1968 a ghostly cat appeared and that faucets would turn on by themselves. But the bulk of his hauntings were associated with a continuous bouncing sound that was heard in the attic and, after discovering a sealed staircase leading to an attic room, Hunter decided to explore more. Opening the door at the top of the staircase, a red ball fell down the stairs, only to vanish after a couple of bounces. Shortly thereafter, Hunter discovered a trunk in the attic containing the journal of a sickly 9-year-old boy. His elaborate story continues from there, painting the picture of a boy kept in the attic when his family discovered he was infirm. As he was heir to a large fortune, the family feared that his death would mean the money would pass on to someone else, so they adopted a child that looked like him, whom they trained to be their own. They secretly buried their real son when he died. Hunter claims that a séance led him to the burial ground of the boy, but the ghostly activity in the house became more violent after he was uncovered. His story inspired the 1980s film *The Changeling*. Historian Phil Goodstein, however, claims in his book *The Ghosts of Denver: Capitol Hill* that many elements of Hunter's story do not add up, such as the age of the boy and that no one in Colorado had as large a fortune as Hunter described.

Strange occurrences continued to happen after the destruction of the house in the 1970s. Residents complained of large dust clouds, and some found red rubber balls in the street near it. And there are those who claim that the ghost of the child may have followed Hunter to his new home.

CHAPTER 3

Molly Brown House Museum
DENVER

Titanic survivor Molly Brown is one of Colorado's few celebrities. Her historic home holds tours, where she is said to make ghostly appearances.

NOT ALL HAUNTED SPACES HAVE THEIR STORIES soaked in gore, violence, and death. The Molly Brown House Museum, which is possibly haunted by its namesake, provides a good example of this.

Margaret "Molly" Brown did many notable things in her life—the most famous of which was surviving the sinking of RMS *Titanic* in 1912. Arguably one of Colorado's most beloved celebrities, she left her mark on the Mile High City in many ways. Better known for her unofficial nickname, "The Unsinkable Molly Brown," she inspired both a musical and later a film starting Debbie Reynolds in the '60s. According to one of the Molly Brown House Museum's tour guides, Catherine Trumpis, the fiery and passionate woman never went by Molly in her lifetime, just Margaret or Maggie. Impressions she left on the world go beyond her sense of spirit, her activism, and the tragedy of the *Titanic*. Her house, now a historic landmark and museum, may hold her ghost as well.

She was born Margaret Tobin in Hannibal, Missouri, in 1867. Her family was very poor, and Margaret dropped out of school in the eighth grade to help care for her five brothers and sisters. During my tour of the Molly Brown House Museum on September 18, 2014, Trumpis said that Margaret made her way to Leadville, Colorado, hoping to find a husband after receiving a letter from her brother Daniel, who lived there and alluded to her impending future as a spinster. She would later wed James Joseph "J.J." Brown in 1886. Margaret was 19 when they were married, and J.J. was 32. They had two children while living in Leadville, Lawrence and Catherine.

Although they married poor, J.J. would later help create a technique to shore up mine walls. This enabled his mining venture, Ibex Mining Company, to hit what was the largest gold strike at the time in Colorado, the Little Johnny Mine. As a reward, he was given shares of company stock, and the Browns bought and moved into their home at 1340 Pennsylvania St. in Denver 1894 after coming into this fortune. They purchased the house for $30,000, the equivalent today of about $833,300. Unlike many

Victorian homes of the period, their house had electricity, a phone, three central heating units, and indoor plumbing.

Once the Browns had settled into their home in Capitol Hill, Margaret started throwing parties to take part in the higher society that Denver offered. Allegedly, J.J. did not approve of these parties and would spend all his time during them in his study smoking cigars. This leads to the first item on the list of possible hauntings in the house: the lingering smell of cigars. Although no one has been allowed to smoke in any area of the house for several years, guests of the museum's daily tours have noticed the odor of cigars, specifically on the second floor where J.J.'s study was. It should also be noted that while J.J. and Margaret's mother, Johanna Collins Tobin, enjoyed smoking, Margaret herself did not, saying it smoked up the house and that she did not like the smell. In 1910 she converted J.J.'s smoking parlor where he entertained guests into a library.

A big reason Margaret was able to convert J.J.'s parlor was because the couple had separated in 1909. The couple never formally divorced due to their religion, but they never reconciled either. Trumpis said that their relationship may have crumbled due to Margaret's activism for miner's rights, to which J.J., who served as a mining official, was in direct opposition. While Margaret's campaigns may have caused some of their marital issues, Trumpis also mentioned that J.J. was frequently seen with other women.

Once Margaret had separated from J.J. she began to travel the world. Aside from her house on Pennsylvania Street in Denver, she had homes in Lakewood, Colorado, and Newport, Rhode Island, and an apartment in New York City. She was in Cairo, Egypt, with her daughter during one of her many trips abroad when she received a telegram from her son, Larry, saying her first grandchild was very ill. She decided to head back to the United States on the first vessel on which she could obtain passage: the *Titanic.*

Most know the background of the sinking of the *Titanic,* and some even know Margaret's role aboard it, as a result of James Cameron's 1997 film, in which actress Kathy Bates played this chapter's heroine. When Margaret discovered the chaos above deck while the ship was sinking on April 14, 1912, she immediately took control. She began ushering people onto lifeboats and, according to Trumpis, did not get on one herself until forced by some of the ship's crewmen. She was put onto lifeboat six, which was filled with 24 passengers, less than half of its 65-person capacity. Twenty-one of the lifeboat's passengers were women and the other three were men. Among those men was the one who actually steered the *Titanic* into the fatal iceberg, Quartermaster Robert Hichens. According to Trumpis, originally there were only two men aboard the lifeboat, but a third was added because Hichens refused to do anything.

Some accounts say that as people in the lifeboats watched the *Titanic* crack and finally sink, several passengers jumped from the sinking ship into the frozen waters below. Where accounts differ is whether or not Margaret had the men rowing her lifeboat go to help those people. Other lifeboats did not go to the aid of the people in the water because they feared the sinking *Titanic* would pull the smaller vessels under with it. While there is no record of whether Margaret was able to save any people in the water, many attribute the "unsinkable" part of her nickname to her brave attempt. Once the ship had sunk and the survivors were picked up by RMS *Carpathia,* Margaret was put in charge of the survivors' committee on the trip back to New York. She was picked for several reasons: People were able to relate to her spiritually as a Catholic in their time of grief; she was fluent in English, German, Russian, and French; and, finally, she was skilled at fundraising. In fact, she was able to raise $10,000

The library in the Molly Brown House was used more frequently by Brown's husband, who favored cigars. Allegedly, the smell of cigars can be detected within the house even though smoking has not been allowed for some time.

before the survivors disembarked in New York. Upon her return to New York, reporters asked why she did not sink with the *Titanic,* and Margaret is reported to have answered, "Hell, I'm unsinkable." The rest, as they say, is history.

Margaret's amazing story continues from there. She volunteered as a nurse with the Red Cross in 1917 during World War I, which earned her a French Legion of Honor medal. One of the other notable things that she did in her life was to help create a juvenile court system in Colorado. She also ran for a seat in the senate three times, all before women had the right to vote, and she was one of the first women to do so, with a campaign that promoted domestic rights for women and children. She also acted on the stage in London and Paris.

During tours of the Molly Brown House Museum, guests can walk through almost the entire home, with the exception of the third floor, where she used to throw parties. Several of the hauntings, though, actually occur on the second floor of the house, including the aforementioned cigar smoke smell from J.J.'s study. Another common episode involves a rocking chair that sits in what used to be Margaret's room, which several people claim to have seen rocking back and forth of its own accord. Daily tours take place approximately every 30 minutes during the museum's operating hours. The museum also hosts special exhibits pertaining to Margaret's history, as well as special Halloween tours—called Victorian Horrors—and other holiday events. Guests of tours have also claimed to see apparitions that looked exactly like portraits of Margaret that are found throughout the house. One guest even claims that the ghost of Margaret kindly, albeit silently, pointed her in the direction of the bathroom.

"Mrs. Margaret Tobin Brown lived in this house during the Victorian era, which was a time when people were obsessed with spiritualism," said Museum Director Andrea Malcomb. She also talked about some of the things Victorian-era people would do to attract ghosts, such as conducting séances, consulting with psychics, and using Ouija boards. She added that, while the museum prefers to concentrate on what Margaret Brown did during her lifetime, psychics have conducted their own investigations there.

"There have been independent psychics who have visited the museum who claim that Mrs. Brown's mother, Johanna Tobin, roams the second floor, that J.J. smokes cigars in the back hallway, and that a maid is dusting the library shelves," Malcomb said.

After Margaret's death in 1932, the house was sold for $5,000 (approximately $86,200 today). During the time of the Great Depression, people in the city were selling houses for anything they could get, according to Trumpis. The house would later change hands several times, even becoming a home for wayward girls in the 1960s. In the early '70s, the city looked at demolishing the house in favor of something new and more urban. This is when the idea of Colorado's Landmark Preservation was born. The organization Historic Denver was created and purchased the home in 1970, making it the organization's flagship property. The Molly Brown House Museum would become the first home to gain landmark status (ordinance number 113, March 30, 1971).

When the home was first purchased in 1970 for use as a museum, none of the Browns' original belongings were still in it, and the girls home had updated the kitchen to 1960s standards. Fortunately, Margaret not only loved to throw parties, but she also loved to take pictures of them to share with friends who could not make it. Trumpis said the museum now has several pieces of the Browns' original furniture thanks to the curators' use of these photos. Trumpis also mentioned that none of the items in the house are younger than 1910; she estimated that the curators were able to obtain 35%–40% of the Browns' original belongings that were in the house.

In the absence of violence, the Molly Brown House Museum has acquired the ghost of a fiery, strong woman, and maybe the occasional sign of disapproval from her husband. But her presence does beg the question of what makes her stay. Maybe she feels as if her work of fighting for the rights of others is not yet over. More than likely, of course, we will never know.

CHAPTER 4

Oxford Hotel

DENVER

Several rooms in the oldest hotel in Denver are reportedly haunted.

AS THE OLDEST HOTEL IN DENVER, the Oxford
Hotel's history is rooted in luxury. Built in 1891 during the peak
of the silver rush, the hotel was fitted with gas heating and an
elevator and even had its own power plant to enable these luxuries. It was, in fact, one of the first buildings in Denver to have
elevators, or as they were better known then, "vertical railways."
With an ideal location of mere blocks away from the railway at
Union Station, rooms would set weary travelers back $1, or $2 if
they wanted a bath. This was made possible because each floor
had its own water closets and other sanitary appliances.

At the time the hotel opened, Denver was considered the third largest city in the West after San Francisco and Omaha. The hotel survived the Silver Panic that caused many businesses to crumble in 1893, and it continued to thrive. Its subsequent history includes several renovations and additions to the building.

The start of a new century did not halt the hotel's booming business. In 1902, hotel manager Calvin Morse boasted that the hotel was so popular that it was hosting 35,000 guests per year and they were turning people away due to no vacancies. This popularity led to the first addition to the hotel, a two-story building behind the hotel on Wazee Street. Not much later, in 1906, the new managers conducted a remodel of the hotel that added an exterior entrance to the barbershop, a mezzanine, a café, and marble wainscoting (decorative paneling). In 1912, a five-story annex was added, connected to the original hotel by a bridge from its second story. Since being renovated once again in the 1930s, the Oxford has been known for its Art Deco style. This renovation also added the Cruise Room, the hotel's local watering hole.

In 1979, the hotel gained a new owner, who temporarily closed it for renovations. This round of changes turned out to be quite important, as the owners discovered false ceilings and other unexplored areas of the property. They found several items in these hidden rooms, including blueprints from the first architect, which helped the renovations more closely match the original work. This was also when they began to modernize the hotel and the era during which it attained landmark status. For those who dare to look, there are also a few gems of ghostly activity hidden throughout the building's many stylish rooms.

The building was designed by Frank E. Edbrooke, who, coincidentally, designed the Brown Palace, Denver's second oldest hotel and the Oxford's prime competition for the most haunted hotel in Denver. The hotel is five stories high and contains several reputedly haunted locations.

One of the first haunted locations presents a little bit of a novelty. Located off the main lobby and down some stairs on a lower floor is a women's restroom, but when the hotel was originally built, this area was the barbershop. Some of the activity here is fairly "typical," such as doors locking by themselves and faucets turning on of their own accord. What makes this restroom a little more unique is that the ghost who resides there is apparently a peeping tom who has frightened several women trying to use the facilities. Undoubtedly, this puts the hotel in a slight predicament, as there are not many women who would appreciate a desk clerk telling them that the person startling them in the bathroom is a ghost or a figment of their imagination.

The next room that sees ghostly activity is the Cruise Room. It now houses Denver's first post-Prohibition bar, which opened the day after passage of the 21st Amendment, which ended Prohibition in December 1933. On the more racy side of history, there is rumor that before the Cruise Room officially opened, it was the location of a speakeasy, complete with a secret back stair that led to a room with prostitutes. As far as paranormal activity goes, it is reputed to be haunted by the ghost of an old man who comes to the bar to order a beer. Bartenders and patrons alike have witnessed the man drink his beer and continuously mutter about getting presents to children. When the man leaves and the bartender goes to pick up his empty glass, however, he always finds it full again. He is supposedly the ghost of a mailman who was going to deliver Christmas presents to children in Central City in the early 1900s, but he never arrived, and people assumed he had stolen the gifts. His partially frozen and decomposed body, however, was found in Central City with the presents still with him near the end of winter.

One of the more mystifying and scary areas of the Oxford Hotel is its attic. It used to be a hot spot for ghost tours but now the hotel uses it for storage, and customers are no longer allowed

into it. Some say it is one of the more eerie of the haunted locations in the building, and it has been the subject of paranormal
investigations in which people claim to have recorded voices. Some
employees will not go up into the attic alone because of the creepy
vibes they get there. There have also been reports of objects stored
there moving by themselves and the distinct sounds of footsteps
behind people when it is obvious no one else is there.

The last of the haunted locations in the Oxford Hotel is room
320. About half of the stories about it say that a woman named
Florence Richardson was staying in the hotel with her husband
one night in 1898 when she decided to kill him and then turn
the gun on herself. There is no proof that the couple were actually married, but they registered for the room as "H. C. Rockwell
and wife" from Greeley, Colorado. She shot him and then herself
a half hour later. The name H. C. Rockwell was presumed to
be an alias, as the man Richardson shot was later identified as
W. H. Lawrence from Cleveland, Ohio. *The New York Times* ran
an article on the deaths of both Lawrence and Richardson on
September 12, 1898, citing jealousy as the motive for the killing,
but the article did not provide the room number. The other half
of the accounts say that a man caught his wife with another man
in this room and killed them both, which fits better with the
paranormal experiences people have had in the room. Indeed,
the ghostly presence seems to make itself known only when there
is a single man staying there, and the men have reported waking
up to an apparition of a male figure at the foot of the bed yelling
about corrupting his wife. Reportedly this has caused several of
the men to leave the room, and in turn the hotel, immediately.
Other accounts report the bathroom light turning on and off
very quickly and feeling a depression in the bed next to the guest
as if someone were lying down.

Room 320 has been called the Murder Room and is one of
the most requested in the hotel. Like the attic, it has also had

Strangler's Row

Before the Lower Downtown (LoDo) area became the long strip of bars and restaurants it is today, it was filled with businesses of a different kind. When the city was founded, present-day Market Street was called McGaa Street after William McGaa who, after General William Larimer (who helped found the city of Denver), was responsible for naming streets. However, he soon became known as the town drunk and the city founders voted for a name change. Benjamin Holladay was the next man to have the street named in his honor. His claim to the right was that he had picked Denver over Auraria to be the main station for the stagecoach in the 1860s. When the street started to be filled with brothels, however, the Holladay family petitioned for its name to be changed so they would not be associated with the newly founded red-light district. Their request was granted and the name changed to Market Street, which it is still called today. For some time during its brothel days, Market Street began to be known by a different name due to a series of murders that the paper likened to England's Jack the Ripper. Indeed, some papers called the murderer Jack the Strangler, and this was how Market Street got the unfortunate nickname "Strangler's Row."

In 1894, papers across the United States were buzzing about three murders that had happened in Denver, specifically on the west side of the 1900 block of Market Street. All three women were prostitutes, and all three were left dead in their beds with no signs of struggle. First killed was 37-year-old Lena Trapper (1911 Market St.), next was 23-year-old Marie Constassot (1925 Market St.), and last was a woman suspected to be in her 20s named

Kiku Oyama (1975 Market St.). The three women were killed in a short time frame, within a few days of each other, according to *The Atlanta Constitution* in a November 16, 1894, article called "Denver's Great Murder Mystery." The murderer came in, most likely posing as a customer, and silently strangled them. There were no known witnesses, although another prostitute reportedly saw a man leaving the building in a hurry after the death of Oyama. Supposedly, a clairvoyant also came to the police after the murders and used her abilities to provide a description of the killer. Some of the details she gave to the police matched several details they had already found in their investigations, such as describing an item taken from Oyama by the killer.

Because of the lack of witnesses, no one was actually charged with the murders of these women, although many men were arrested. According to *The New York Times*, an Italian man was arrested after he was caught in the act of strangling a woman named Marie Anderson; however, the police thought he was not the real strangler but a copycat.

Despite arrests being made, the women of Denver were still terrified, and many of those working in the brothels were worried the Strangler would strike again. Some of the working girls also started to claim that they had seen the ghost of Trapper in buildings near where she had been murdered. After Oyama's death, however, the Strangler disappeared and no more women were murdered. To this day the question of what happened to Jack the Strangler remains unanswered.

many paranormal investigators visit it. Another thing that is different about this room is that it is the only one with a decorative plaque on the headboard. This brass plaque reads: "Come sweet dreams; the hour of sweet beguile." Research indicates this passage is fairly close to the English translation of the French poem "The Child Asleep" by Clotilde de Surville, which reads "Sweet error! He but slept, I breathe again / Come gentle dreams, the hour of sleep beguile! / Oh when shall he, for whom I sigh in vain / Beside me watch to see thy waking smile." No one is sure why this room in particular has this embellishment.

Two friends of mine actually worked at the Oxford Hotel, and both occasionally worked graveyard shifts during their employment. In addition to confirming most of the above ghost stories, they had some of their own to add as well. They preferred not to be mentioned by name, but one of them, who worked at the hotel for more than five years, participated in several of the haunted tours throughout the hotel as well as a séance in room 320. During one of the tours he took a mother and daughter up to the attic to take pictures with their digital camera. The first couple of images showed just a couple of orbs, but the next one showed hundreds in the same spot. He said it felt as if the spirits had all rallied into the room because they were there taking photos. Both employees said that the theory behind the haunting in the attic is that it was originally divided into rooms for the overflow of soldiers staying there during times of war, some of whom were sick and injured and may have died there. The other employee mentioned that visitors to the attic can see the divisions where the different rooms were.

Both of my friends also claim that the postman is also not the only ghost that has been seen in the Cruise Room, and the spirit of a little girl has been seen around there and the second floor. One of them mentioned a time that the girl was photographed in the Cruise Room right after opening when there were only two customers at the bar, and they think she may have been the daughter of a prostitute who died in an unknown accident in the hotel. She also said that she got odd vibes walking through the hotel and that when she would do rounds of the building at night she would sometimes hear voices from rooms she knew were empty.

One of the last things the two mentioned was a suicide that happened in a room on the second floor. While nothing incredibly out of the ordinary happens in the room itself, there is an orb that continually seems to fall out of the second story window from which the man threw himself. According to the pair, the hotel currently no longer advertises itself as a haunted hotel and has stopped giving haunted tours, although CBS did rate it as one of the top haunted tours in 2012. The hotel may no longer present itself as a haunted getaway, but customers still flock to room 320 and the rest of the site, hoping to catch a glimpse of past lodgers who never left.

CHAPTER 5

Denver's Infamous Brothels

DENVER

The Navarre building, which is now a museum, used to house a brothel. Its location directly across the street from one of Denver's most prestigious hotels caused some problems for businessmen who did not want to be seen going from one place to the other. Tunnels underneath the buildings helped to solve that problem.

BAR BRAWLS AND LOOSE WOMEN are indelibly part of the history of the Old West and, once Denver was established, it too had a red-light district. Some of these brothels became connected to expensive hotels via an intricate underground tunnel system that was built beneath the Mile High City, as its wealthy did not want to be seen coming and going from such establishments. Rumor has it that these passageways were put to further use during Prohibition, and many businesses used them to transport liquor and sometimes trade it with brothels. While the tunnels still exist underneath Denver, they are not widely used, many of them have been closed down, and some, like those underneath the capitol building, are used for storage. One of the brothels on this tunnel system could be found across the street from the Brown Palace Hotel, connecting the hotel to one of the city's top businesses for ladies of the night.

THE NAVARRE

THIS BUILDING WAS ORIGINALLY BUILT as a school for girls in 1880 and was called the Brinker Collegiate Institute. While originally it served only women, it soon after became a coed institution. After the death of the school's namesake in 1889, the building was sold and reopened as Hotel Richelieu, a more infamous type of establishment. Here gentlemen could dine with ladies of the night, either publicly or in more private areas of the building.

The thought process behind this idea was that there was a pool of clients just across the street, but business did not take off quite as quickly as its owners might have hoped. As noted, to be seen coming to and from The Navarre from the Brown was not ideal for a gentleman, and that was how the idea for the tunnel system was born. The first tunnel connected the basement of the Brown Palace Hotel to the Hotel Richelieu around 1892. Later, a whole system of tunnels would spread underneath Denver, connecting other hotels and even the government buildings of the city to the whorehouses.

Today, buildings can tap into the tunnels for hot or cold air, an unlikely heating and cooling system that is sold by the city of Denver. Bryan Bonner and Matthew Baxter of the Rocky Mountain Paranormal Research Society (RMPRS) said that due to movement of air, the tunnels can make a plethora of ghostlike sounds. They also said that, unfortunately, some of the tunnels are too dangerous to go into, and many have also been closed down or sealed. With the help of the tunnel, the Navarre became the second-best brothel in the city, after Mattie's House of Mirrors—which, incidentally, is also considered to be haunted (see next page).

Many of the ghosts believed to reside in The Navarre, predominantly on the second floor, are said to be those of the working girls. Bonner said that on one of RMPRS's ghost tours, a guest allegedly saw someone pull back a curtain while the group was standing in front of The Navarre. He said it was unlikely anyone was working in the building at the time, as it is now the home of the American Museum of Western Art—the Anschutz Collection. As all of the RMPRS tours are done at night and after business hours for the museum, only security personnel should have been in the building and, according to Bonner, they never leave their posts. His theory is that the mysterious figure who pulled back the curtain may have been the ghost of a working girl.

The building continued to be used as a brothel until the early 1900s, when it became home to a different kind of discouraged business: gambling. In fact, the building's current name, The Navarre, came about after the building was lost in a card game. The new owner named the building for a French king. One of the building's ghost stories is that of a man who was not gambling well one night and decided to pull his gun and shoot himself in the chest for everyone to see. It is said that visitors can hear him wandering the halls on the lower floor.

After the city began clearing out gambling halls and brothels, the building became a fine restaurant and eventually a top jazz club in the city. It was purchased in 1997 by the Anschutz Corporation. Regardless of who owns it, however, the RMPRS leaders say it is a good idea to keep an eye on The Navarre, as it currently seems to have a lot of ghostly activity happening in it.

MATTIE'S HOUSE OF MIRRORS

THE HOUSE OF MIRRORS BUILDING was built by Jennie Rogers in 1889 (and is today Lodo's Bar and Grill). Rogers's primary objective for the brothel was to compete with Mattie Silks, another brothel owner in Denver. When the building first opened it was located on Holladay Street, which within a few years was renamed Market Street. In 1894, before Rogers opened for business, the brothels were shaking in their boots after the murders of three prostitutes on Market, which became known as Strangler's Row as a result.

Rogers ran the brothel until 1910. Silks then came in and the two ran the brothel together for a short time. During their ghost tour, Bonner and Baxter talk about one of the rumors, or urban legends as they refer to it, surrounding the competitive pair and how many people think Silks wanted the building so badly she challenged Rogers to a topless sword fight for ownership of it. Bonner and Baxter insist this is strictly a legend, albeit a fun one.

In any event, once Silks was in control of the building, she converted the lower floor into a respectable restaurant. The building gained its name, the House of Mirrors, because any and all surfaces were covered in mirrors. The upstairs was a little less family-friendly than the restaurant. Customers would go up to their rooms and, once they closed the doors, could pull down Murphy beds from the wall that, when lowered, blocked the doors, effectively locking them and making it impossible for anyone to come in. The cost was 75 cents for a girl in a regular room, and $2.50 for a room that included heat.

While there are plenty of rumors about people who have died in the building, the RMPRS could find the record for the death of only one woman. Ella Wellington was at one point an owner of the building, but in addition to that she may have also been an accountant or working girl there as well. Wellington's cause of death is also an open question; the three most popular possibilities include homicide by an upset customer, homicide by an equally upset boyfriend, or suicide in front of a local politician.

In 2000, the RMPRS investigated the building. Some of the reports of ghostly activity come from the room where Wellington died but are not limited to that room. Some of the reported activity includes a piano playing by itself, the elevator moving between floors when it had not been called, and the smell of smoke in the bathrooms. Several people also reported hearing parties when no one was in the building. Several staff members refuse to go to the upstairs area of Mattie's alone. During this investigation, RMPRS was able to pick up what sounded like a conversation between two voices in a corner; a writeup of what the group experienced, along with the recorded conversation, can be found on its website (along with those of other buildings it has investigated).

One of the other reports the group investigated in the building came from a night manager who noticed that in one of the back rooms, lights would dim and then brighten in time with his breathing. This would also stop when he held his breath. The manager quit that very night. In this particular room, it is rumored that one of the working girls' boyfriends committed suicide, but there is no existing record of this occurring. Baxter and Bonner said, however, that it is possible there were deaths other than Wellington's in the building, as record keeping was notoriously bad at the time. As part of their investigation of this specific activity, the RMPRS monitored all the lights from the room in question that were on the same circuit. Baxter said the reason for this is that all lights on the same electric circuit should behave the same way because they are using the same current. During its investigation, the RMPRS recorded video of only one of the lights on the circuit fluctuating between dim and bright. They claim that while this video was being recorded,

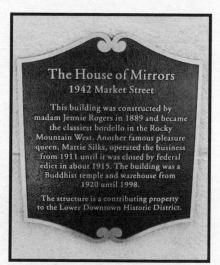

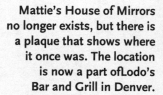

Mattie's House of Mirrors
no longer exists, but there is
a plaque that shows where
it once was. The location
is now a part ofLodo's
Bar and Grill in Denver.

both Baxter and Bonner were downstairs discussing the alleged
suicide of the boyfriend, but they cannot say for sure whether
the activity was happening because of their discussion. As part
of their ghost tour, they also mention that the electric wiring
has been redone three times in the building since the 1980s
and that no problem with the wiring has been found that would
cause this sort of activity to happen. Additionally, the two buildings on either side are on the same power grid and have never
reported any problems of this nature. Baxter also said that he
has witnessed the lights do this on multiple occasions.

During Silks's time running the building, it earned the reputation of being one of the finest gentleman's places in Denver.
She even offered her working girls benefits, such as higher pay
and medical attention. The restaurant had a strong reputation as
well. Silks ran the building until 1915, when the city of Denver's
morals got the best of the business and several brothels in the
area, including Mattie's House of Mirrors, were shut down. The
building is now a restaurant and bar, where, during a renovation, the decorative mirrors were removed.

CHAPTER 6

Brown Palace Hotel

DENVER

The Brown Palace Hotel in Denver competes with the Oxford Hotel (which is also supposedly haunted) as the oldest hotel in the city.

COMPLETED IN THE SUMMER OF 1892 and designed by the same architect who brought Denver the Oxford Hotel, the Brown Palace has hosted some of the nation's most elite. Its roster includes British Invasion band The Beatles along with every president since Teddy Roosevelt, with the exception of Calvin Coolidge. Located on the corner of 17th Street and Tremont Place, the triangle-shaped building is eye-catching, and maybe even haunted.

Henry Cordes Brown came to Denver in 1860, working initially as a carpenter but ultimately developing and contracting the land that he had been homesteading. His first claim to fame would be selling his land to the city so that Colorado could have its capitol built there, and the rest of his fortune was made by selling the remainder of his land bit by bit. He was considered the wealthiest man in Colorado by 1880, and the area would eventually become Capitol Hill.

Reportedly, the Windsor Hotel, a luxurious hotel in Del Norte, Colorado, had not let Brown enter because of his attire. Determined to outdo the Windsor, he built the Brown Palace. The hotel was fashioned in Italian Renaissance style, had balconies up to the eighth floor, and had the first atrium-style lobby in the nation. Onyx was imported from Mexico for the lobby as well as for the eighth floor ballroom, and the Onyx Room—previously called the Grand Salon—on the second floor. Because no wood was used in the construction of the building, it was hailed as the second fireproof building in America (after the County Records Building in South Carolina). Upon opening, the hotel had 400 rooms (compared to the current count of 241), and they cost between $3 and $5 a night. In addition, the hotel has an artesian well beneath it that still provides all the water to the building today. The building cost $1.6 million, plus another $400,000 to furnish it, a little more than $42 million in current dollars. The hotel also boasts that, since opening, it has never closed its doors.

Unlike the Oxford Hotel, which began to steer away from the stigma of being haunted, the Brown Palace Hotel continues to embrace the idea. During Halloween weekend of 2014, it offered a Spirits with Spirit package that included a ghost tour of the hotel with mediums. It also had a package for the month of October called Enduring Guests at the Brown and provided guests with a brochure they could use to give themselves self-guided tours of the hotel. With a long string of ghost stories to choose from, guests were sure to be set for Halloween.

Our ghost stories for this chapter start with a Denver socialite named Louise Crawford Hill. Called Louise Sneed when she came from North Carolina in 1893 as an aspiring social climber in search of a husband, she met Crawford Hill while visiting cousins in Denver. They were married in 1895 and would have two sons, Crawford Jr. and Nathaniel Peter IV. Once married, Louise decided to take over Denver's upper-class society, and the couple built a mansion on 10th Avenue and Sherman Street.

After this home was completed, Louise invited who she thought were the top 36 women in Denver society and they came to be known as the Sacred Thirty-Six. It is rumored that Margaret "Molly" Brown strove to be invited into this group once she came into her fortune, but was never allowed into it. This story led to Louise's being immortalized as the evil character in the musical "The Unsinkable Molly Brown."

In 1914, Louise met Buckeley Wells, with whom she started having an affair. This situation seemed to be tolerated by her husband, as the three would sometimes dine and go out together. Wells's wife, on the other hand, did not approve, and the two divorced in 1918. Four years later, Crawford died. Louise thought that Wells would marry her after she became a widow, but instead he ran away and eloped with another woman. Upon hearing this news, Louise decided to ruin Wells financially—the phrase "Hell hath no fury like a woman scorned" comes to mind. By 1931, Wells was on the verge of bankruptcy after Louise convinced several of his financial backers to pull their support. He committed suicide the same year.

The luxury of the Brown Palace Hotel is perhaps the reason spirits find the building so appealing. Louise Crawford Hill, one of the ghosts who allegedly haunts it, was quite the socialite in Denver while she was alive.

After the death of her husband, Louise began living in the Brown Palace Hotel due to the difficulty of obtaining domestic help to care for her mansion during the second World War. She occupied a suite in the hotel from 1942 to 1955.

Once, when the hotel was giving a ghost tour, the group stopped in front of what was Louise's room to tell her story, describing her life as one of heartbreak, as she became a recluse after Wells's death and during her years in the hotel. Almost immediately after, the front desk began receiving phone calls from the room, but the operator heard nothing but static upon answering. This was especially strange, as the room was closed for renovation at the time and did not have a guest staying in it. In addition, the phone line had been taken out of the room during the renovation. This continued until hotel management decided to remove the room from the tours, after which the strange calls ceased. According to the Rocky Mountain Paranormal Research Society's frontmen, Bryan Bonner and Matthew Baxter, however, there are a number of problems with this story.

"We did a little more research and discovered, well, there was never actually a telephone line installed in her room, which either discredits it completely or makes it the creepiest ghost story I've ever heard. Not too sure which," Bonner said.

Another rumored ghost is a woman who appears on the sixth floor. She always appears to be crying and her face is streaked with tears. Some say you can also hear her crying at night, even though her ghost is nowhere to be seen. It is said that it may be the ghost of Sarah Hall, a woman who stayed at the hotel in 1914 and was engaged to a man named Herbert Crabtree. During her visit, she received a telegram concerning Crabtree. He had recently taken passage to England to collect a fortune given to him by an uncle in his will, sailing on RMS *Empress of Ireland* from Quebec, Canada. Sadly, this ship sank on the voyage after colliding with SS *Storstad* in the Saint Lawrence River, and more than two-thirds of the passengers were killed, including Hall's dear fiancé. Upon receiving the telegram bearing this bad news, it is said that Hall went to her suite, bathed, and then dressed for a special occasion, including perfume and her best jewelry. She then hanged herself from the chandelier with a note that said "I've gone to join Herbert."

Other than saddened women, the Brown Palace Hotel reputedly has other ghosts that roam its halls. During its early years, for example, there was a room where guests could buy train tickets. Allegedly, spectral conductors and train passengers alike, complete with luggage, can be seen in the room; both are given away by their period clothes.

In addition, the dining room, now called Ellyngtons, used to be known as the San Marco Room. Here, guests could enjoy social gatherings and music, and it was often used as a concert hall for big bands and the San Marco Strings. Although many bands played in this room throughout the history of the hotel, one supposedly never left the building and its ghostly members still practice here, dressed and ready for a show. Upon seeing a group of three practicing in the concert hall one night, an employee reportedly said that they were not allowed to be in the room at that hour, to which one of the band members replied, "Don't worry; we live here" before vanishing.

According to Bonner and Baxter's ghost tour, there is also the ghost of a young woman who killed herself by jumping down the stairs that led from the atrium area and take a right angle into the lobby. This happened in the early 1900s, and reportedly both guests and employees have seen this suicide repeated as the woman tumbles down the stairs.

Other ghostly activity throughout the hotel includes papers flying off of desks mysteriously, doors slamming shut, cold spots, flickering lights, and the sounds of children playing and laughing in the halls. There are other full apparitions of ghosts in the hotel as well. There is an old woman who comes to complain of the cold in her room but vanishes once an employee comes to help. Some have reported sightings of a frontier-era prostitute, as well as a former bellhop who takes newspapers away from in front of people's rooms. Finally, people have claimed to see Brown himself pacing the hallways before disappearing into one of the walls. In 1893, the silver market crashed, and many a wealthy person in Denver fell with it, including Brown. Although his grand hotel had been open for a full year at that point, he was having difficulty paying his debts. To avoid the inevitable foreclosure, Brown sold his mortgage for the hotel for $600,000 plus the guarantee that he could live in it for the rest of his life. The presence of his ghost, however, suggests that he dedicated more than just his lifetime to the property.

CHAPTER 7

Tivoli Student Union

DENVER

IN THE HEART OF DENVER lies the Auraria Campus, a unique site that is the home of not one, not two, but three college institutions. Both the University of Colorado at Denver and the Metropolitan State University of Denver (provide students with undergraduate- and graduate-level education, while the Community College of Denver awards associate degrees. Auraria, the name of which is derived from the Latin word for gold, is unique to the location as well, as it was the first city in what became first the territory and then the state of Colorado. Denver was founded not long after and expanded to eventually swallow Auraria. The campus is in the area where part of the original city used to be.

On the campus is a building known as the Tivoli Student Union, but it was not always a part of the college site and was originally a brewery. Much of the old equipment used to make beer can still be found inside.

The history of the Tivoli Brewing Company dates all the way back to the start of Denver and the state of Colorado itself. It was originally called Sigi's Brewery in 1864, as it was started by a German man named Moritz Sigi. There is still a pool hall and "cabaret" called Sigi's Pool Hall in the lower level of the student union. The brewery served the community that resided near it, which included the Ninth Street neighborhood, a historic section of houses still on campus with a bar, now called the Tap Room. It now hosts offices for the schools. The community was also home to several immigrant communities, the roots of which still appear on campus. St. Cajetan's was the church for the Hispanic community, the Emmanuel Gallery was originally

The Tivoli was an old beer-brewing company but was shut down. It is now part of the Auraria Campus and is home to several offices and student services for the three colleges on the campus. It recently reopened as a brewery.

the first synagogue in the Denver area, and St. Elizabeth's is the only one of the three churches on campus that still functions as such and holds a Catholic Mass every day.

In 1900, a man named John Good bought the brewery and renamed it Tivoli, and he kept the company afloat during Prohibition by selling a low-alcohol beer called Dash. The brewery thrived in the decades that followed, and in the 1950s it was one of the largest in the United States. It began to struggle in the 1960s due to difficulties with both the economy and the business, and the market for beer had also become much more competitive in Colorado after the opening of the Coors Brewery. A labor strike and severe flooding caused the brewery to stop production for several months, and it eventually closed fully in 1969. It was the second-oldest continuously running brewery in the country. In 2014, a new company called the Tivoli Distributing Company began remaking the beer at the original location and selling it at the Tap Room on campus.

After the brewery closed, the building began to change hands and was even a mall of sorts at one point. In August 1972 it became a national landmark (ordinance 329). The campus was founded in the '70s, which helped boost the economy in the area. A company from San Diego purchased the Tivoli and began to develop it in the 1980s. During its lifetime, the Tivoli had become a mass of 19 buildings with no similar architectural style, and this development group was responsible for combining the buildings and modernizing them. The new and improved Tivoli building, however, was never fully leased with restaurants or stores as they had hoped, and their target clientele tended to favor the more popular downtown area. Then, in 1991, the students of the Auraria Campus voted to buy back the Tivoli and redevelop it for educational purposes. In 1994 the brewery was converted into the campus student union, which included student lounges, a bookstore, a food court, and offices from all three schools.

The Auraria Campus, in the heart of the Denver area, is deeply rooted in the history of the city. Ninth Street Park, a historic neighborhood on campus, is supposedly haunted by some of its early residents.

Before I ever knew the stories of the haunted Tivoli, like most of the students on campus I frequented the building. For two years, I worked on the third floor of the Tivoli, in MSU Denver's Office of Student Media. I started as a reporter and eventually became an editor for the school's newspaper, *The Metropolitan*. Every Tuesday during that time, with the exception of school breaks, I would be in room 313 helping to put the last touches on the newest issue of the paper with the rest of the staff. We would often be there until the wee hours of the morning.

During those nights, the cleaning staff would turn off the lights in the rest of the building after a point. When leaving the office to run to the bathroom, even the most rational adult could imagine strange sounds as they walked the dark hallway and opened the door to what seemed to be an even darker restroom. Some of the strange occurrences that happened to me in the third-floor bathroom were doors and locks moving by themselves and toilets flushing when there was no one in the stall. The three faucets on the wall would also all turn on simultaneously. I was not the only person from the Student Media Office to experience strange goings-on in the third-floor women's restroom; both the managing editor at the paper and the office manager had experiences similar to mine. The managing editor also claimed to see a face in the mirror on one occasion. After several episodes like this, I decided to use a different bathroom on the first floor in the food court area instead. As I came off the main stairs and was still about 10 feet from the bathroom, however, I heard a toilet flush. When I opened the door, I saw that the room was pitch black and that clearly no one had been in it for some time.

Students and employees alike seem to know that the Tivoli has a reputation and, beyond my personal experiences in the building's restrooms, there are other locations in the Tivoli that are apparently haunted.

Jeff Stamper, assistant vice president for operations and services for the Auraria Higher Education Center, has worked on campus for 24 years and was a student there before that. Most of his time has been spent working in the Tivoli and, in fact, he was the Student Union Director before assuming his current position. Before becoming the director, however, Stamper was a "low person on the totem pole" and would often close the Tivoli during his shifts or after events. He was closing the building on one such occasion and, as this was before the campus had a police department, was patrolling to ensure there was no one left in the building. Stamper said he noticed an open exterior door that he had previously closed.

"I went and I closed it again, and I started walking down the hall back to the office area to get my stuff and go on home," Stamper said. "I felt something kind of swirling around me, and I didn't think too much of it. I took a few more steps. The next thing I knew, there was a very distinct blowing or breath on the back of my neck." While Stamper says that this spirit did not seem particularly malevolent, he has heard stories from others about more-daunting entities that have taunted workers in the building. Most such workers become so scared as a result that they refuse to go back to the Tivoli.

One of these taunting spirits is thought to be a man who worked in the Tivoli during its original incarnation as a brewery and included a spot where trains would pull up to deliver grain into a pitlike area. The story is that the train began pumping out grain before the employee was out of the way, and he was driven into the pit and buried in the grain. People say that it is his presence that can be felt in the lower areas of the Tivoli, notably its basement.

Below the food court, in the bowels of the building, lie the catacombs. This basement area of the Tivloi is not typically open to students, and the only time I have ever personally seen it is when I conducted an interview for the newspaper down in an old bar area. Back in its brewery days, the company stored beer in the catacombs. MSU Denver's Crypto Science club has done haunted history tours of the Tivoli, specifically in the basement, in conjunction with the History Club. A fellow student of mine named Katy Deditz was in the catacombs with friends when they heard the distinct sound of someone walking behind them. Once they rushed out of the hall and looked behind them, they discovered that no one was there. Many claim that the daughter of the brewery's founder also haunts the catacombs. Her name was Margaret Sigi, but she is better known as Molly. Many students and school staff have claimed to hear a little girl laughing in the Tivoli, and this is said to be Molly, but it may also be the spirit of a child who died when the Tivoli flooded.

In 2006 the Crypto Science club invited Frontrange Paranormal Investigators to help them investigate paranormal activity in the Tivoli. Because the catacombs are so out of the way of normal daily campus life, they picked this area as their location for cameras and other equipment. At one point, the investigators claim that their camera stopped working, but audio was able to pick up what sounded like metal banging. As soon as the banging stopped, their camera resumed working. In addition to the banging, they also picked up several recordings of electronic voice phenomena (EVP) and experienced severe battery drainage.

The Travel Channel's *Ghost Adventures* with host Zak Bagans also came to look at the Tivoli as part of its episode on the Peabody-Whitehead Mansion, and they also recorded EVP on their visit to the catacombs. Some of the other sounds that people have heard include those of a large group that seems to be having a party on the third floor, which typically emanate from the air vents.

In addition to the basement hauntings, there is said to be the ghost of a sad girl in the multicultural lounge on the main floor. She is the only apparition that people have reported actually seeing in the building, all other activity being limited to sounds and objects. Like most ghosts, however, the image of the girl disappears as soon as anyone approaches it. Whether or not this is Molly or the young girl who died in the flood is open to debate. Beyond this, a conference room near Sigi's that is occasionally used for events is thought to be haunted by a group of American Indian spirits. Staff who set up the room the day before have come back the next day to find things rearranged despite the door being locked.

The range of paranormal activity in the Tivoli shows that the beings and occurrences are as eclectic as the hodgepodge of 19 buildings that comprise the complex. But despite its haunted nature, the building does not bother most students, and many of them nod their heads knowingly as they exchange ghost stories. Others remain oblivious as they nap on couches in the student lounges. No matter what I have heard about the building, it has remained one of my favorite places on campus, and the ghosts just add more character to it.

Front Range

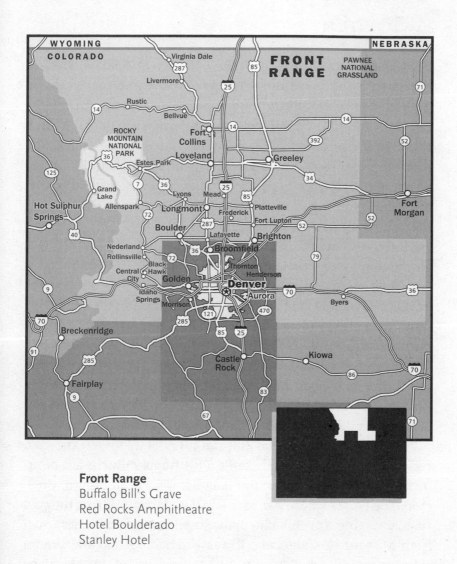

Front Range
Buffalo Bill's Grave
Red Rocks Amphitheatre
Hotel Boulderado
Stanley Hotel

CHAPTER 8

Buffalo Bill's Grave

GOLDEN

BUFFALO BILL AND HIS FAMOUS Wild West show brought a dying breed of frontiersmen back into the limelight. William Frederick "Buffalo Bill" Cody had already garnered a certain amount of fame before pulling this show together and, although it has been nearly 100 years since his death in 1917, controversy still surrounds his burial site on Lookout Mountain in Golden, Colorado. Many argue that he wanted to be buried in Cody, Wyoming, and so his restless spirit may wander this Colorado mountain near his grave.

Buffalo Bill was born in Le Claire, Iowa, on February 26, 1846. He went by many names during his lifetime. His family called him Will; his friends, Billy. During his military career he went by Bill, and he was fondly known as the Colonel in the Wild West show. As a child in Iowa, he played with the American Indians from the area until his family moved to Kansas when he was 8. His father died of scarlet fever when he was 11, and Bill began taking on jobs to support his family, working as a messenger, cattle herder, and wagon train driver at one time or another. As a wagon driver, he crossed the Great Plains on multiple occasions.

Some accounts say that Bill ran away at 13 to join the gold rush in Colorado and also became a fur trapper. By the age of 14, in 1860, he was riding for the Pony Express in Julesburg, Colorado. The Pony Express was a mail service formed during the gold rush, the same year Bill joined, that used horsemen to carry mail from Missouri to California. It was a dangerous job and several riders were killed by Indians. Two years after joining the Pony Express, Bill joined the Seventh Kansas Cavalry and fought for two years in the Civil War on the side of the Union. He returned

Controversy surrounds Buffalo Bill's Grave, as many argue that he should not have been buried in Colorado. While it is said that his last wish was to be buried in Golden, some say he wanted to be buried in Cody, Wyoming, a town named for him. The argument became so strong that the grave was eventually covered in a layer of cement to prevent grave robbers from moving him.

to the West when he was 18 and spent some time scouting for the Army, where he earned the nickname Buffalo Bill.

Upon his return, Bill learned that most of his family had died from illness, and he took care of his remaining sisters thereafter. By the age of 21 he was the chief buffalo hunter and scout for the Kansas Pacific Railroad, feeding more than 1,200 workers with his kills. As his reputation began to grow, so did the rumors of his adventures. Some accounts say that he killed about 11 buffalo per day, or around 4,000 in a year (Bill himself said the number was 4,280). Others noted that he participated in several Indian expeditions but was never harmed. Congress awarded him the Medal of Honor for acts of bravery after helping to defeat the Cheyenne at Summit Springs, Colorado, in 1869.

The same year he was awarded the medal, Buffalo Bill became the subject of dime novels written by Ned Buntline, and legends about him often came from these stories. Taking advantage of his newfound fame, Bill created the Wild West show at the age of 27. At this time, he was married with a son and daughter, and his son died from scarlet fever in 1876. Shortly after his son's death, Bill was called to fight the Cheyenne in Nebraska and killed the tribe's chief, Yellow Hand, during the fight. This very real battle caused a boom in attendance at his Wild West show.

Despite his numerous battles with the Indians, Bill was friends with many of them, and to them he was Pahaska, which means "long hair." Some, such as his friend Sitting Bull, were part of the Wild West show, and when Sitting Bull left the show years later, Bill gave him one of the ponies that could perform tricks.

Buffalo Bill's Wild West show had staged battles with the Indians, stagecoaches, horses, and even a few buffalo. While some say that the large numbers of buffalo killed by Bill helped lead to their near extinction, he helped to revive their population through his show, protecting his herd and breeding them to bring their numbers back up.

The city of Golden is home to Buffalo Bill's Grave and a museum dedicated to his memory. The path to his grave is near steep edges, and supposedly the area is haunted by a tourist who fell and died.

Annie Oakley later became part of the show, and Bill became known as an advocate for women's rights—female performers like her received pay comparable to that of their male counterparts. As the show gained fame, it would even tour parts of Europe, and Queen Victoria of England was reportedly a big fan of it, with the Wild West performing during her Golden Jubilee in 1887.

Once the show had become successful, Bill built a home for his family in Cedar Mountain, Wyoming, a city subsequently named Cody after him. The Wild West show continued running for 30 years but, near the end of his life, Bill was nonetheless running out of money. While staying with his sister in Denver, Bill made a deal with the devil to keep the show running: he took a loan from his friend, Harry Tammen, who was the co-owner of *The Denver Post*. Unfortunately, taking the money came with a price, as Tammen now owned the rights to the show and to the name Buffalo Bill. Tammen's version of the show, Sells Floto Circus, was a mere shadow of Bill's popular one, which caused him to lose more money. Bill reportedly demanded that

Tammen forgive the debt and give him back the show or else Bill would shoot him. There is no record of whether this is true, but allegedly Bill's debt was forgiven. Many, however, claim the stress of this episode hastened his death. He died in his sister's home on January 10, 1917.

Colorado's legislature passed a resolution that his body would sit in the capitol's rotunda until January 14 for viewing, and it is estimated that some 25,000 people came to see it. He would not be buried until June 3, 1917, however, nearly six months after his funeral, and another 20,000 made their way up the mountain to see his grave.

"In Memoriam. Colonel William Frederick Cody. 'Buffalo Bill.' Noted scout, and Indian Fighter. Born February 26, 1856, Scott County, Iowa. Died January 10, 1917, Denver, Colorado," his gravestone reads. Below that it says "At rest here by his request." This is where the controversy comes in, and many people question whether he truly wanted to be buried in Colorado.

Shortly after announcing Bill's death, his sister also stated that he had requested to be buried on Lookout Mountain, a choice that was affirmed by his wife and by the priest who performed last rites for him. This sparked outrage in both Cody, Wyoming, and in North Platte, Nebraska. While North Platte had less of a claim, many people thought Bill would like to be buried there, as it was the site of his first Wild West show. Many residents of Cody, on the other hand, had more of a basis for their fury, and some of them said they had heard Bill himself say multiple times that he would like to be buried in their city. They also said that Bill had written a letter stating his wishes to his sister in 1902 and again, several years later, in his will. Goldie Griffen, a performer in the Wild West show and friend of Bill's, later recorded audio in 1972, four years before she died, saying Bill wished to be buried on Lookout Mountain.

Colorado's fear that residents of Cody would steal Bill's body were high enough that members of the National Guard were present during his open-casket viewing and subsequently at his grave. Later, when Bill's wife died in 1921, she was buried next to him, and their bodies were covered with a layer of concrete, forever making Lookout Mountain their final resting place. The state's fears may have been justified, as there was a $10,000 reward for the body of Buffalo Bill. Some argue that the reason for the change in location was the cost of shipping the body to Wyoming and, because his sister paid the funeral costs, some argue that she had a right to choose his burial site. Others still argue that Tammen bribed Bill's sister into choosing Lookout Mountain.

Both Wyoming and Nebraska have since honored Bill in their own way. The citizens of Cody commissioned a bronze statue that was put on display in 1924, and in 1928 they opened the Cody Memorial Museum. North Platte held a two-day reenactment of the famous Battle of Summit Springs in June 1917, and later that year the town voted to create Cody Park on land that included the area where the first Wild West show had been held.

In 1921, Colorado built the Buffalo Bill Memorial Museum in Golden, near his gravesite. People have reported seeing Bill in the gift shop of the museum and seeing things flying off the shelves or moving. A less reported story relates to the death of a tourist visiting the museum. Allegedly, this woman fell and died, and her ghost can be seen on the mountainside. However, just as people in Cody claim that Bill should have been buried there, they likewise say their museum could be haunted by him as well, and some have reported feeling a presence in the building and museum artifacts coming off the walls. One has to wonder if both places can be haunted by the same man, or if these competing claims simply emanate from urban legends borne from the controversy over Buffalo Bill's final resting place.

CHAPTER 9

Red Rocks Amphitheatre
MORRISON

During the warmer months of summer, you can find people working out at Red Rocks Amphitheatre by day and tailgating at concerts by night. If you pay attention, you may also find the ghost of a miner who haunts the backstage areas of the stadium.

COLORADO IS HOME TO A SECTION of the majestic Rocky Mountains and, as a result, some of the best hiking and skiing in the country. Just a half hour west of Denver, in Morrison, lies Red Rocks Park and Amphitheatre, a personal favorite on my list of places to visit in the state. Geographically, the color of the rocks is unique to one side of the Rocky Mountains and is found in a strip on the east side of the range that extends all the way down to an American Indian reservation in Gallup, New Mexico. With its amphitheatre built into the surrounding rocks, the venue is best known for concerts; The Beatles, U2, the Grateful Dead are just a few of the hundreds that have graced the stage.

The stadium itself holds 9,525 seats. It is also the only outdoor amphitheatre to have naturally perfect acoustics. On either side of the seats are two giant rock monoliths, and the surrounding buildings and restaurants can host weddings and other special events. Hiking trails around the stage area and throughout the park also give people the opportunity for outdoor recreation; during the summer Red Rocks is a popular fitness destination due to the altitude and steep stairs. Events like Yoga on the Rocks and Film on the Rocks keep the area busy with constant crowds in the warm weather and, sometimes, even in the rain.

Although the amphitheatre did not open in its current form until July 1941, people have been using the area for concerts since the early 1900s. John Brisben Walker was one of the first to start bringing performing artists to the area from 1906 to 1910 to give concerts on a temporary platform. In 1927, the manager of Denver Parks, George Cranmer, got Denver to purchase the land from Walker for a little more than $54,000 and convinced the city to continue with Walker's concerts. The federally funded Civilian Conservation Corps and Works Progress Administration became involved and helped to provide labor and materials for the new amphitheatre. Architect Burnham Hoyt decided to use the natural beauty of its surroundings instead of focusing on a man-made stage. The area was formally dedicated on July 15, 1941, and the first of what would become traditional Easter sunrise services took place in 1947.

It seems that the natural beauty of Red Rocks calls to more than just fitness junkies and music lovers. There is, in fact, a spirit in the surrounding area that does not seem to mind the hustle and bustle of the popular venue. Aptly named Hatchet Lady of Red Rocks, she is only one of the ghosts that haunt Red Rocks Park, the 640-acre area that includes the amphitheatre and hiking trails, but her story seems to make her one of the more popular. This is probably because her apparition is that of a headless woman who may have been murdered in the area and who appears to couples getting a little too frisky in the shadows of the rocks. Another theory is that she is the ghost of a woman who homesteaded in the area that became Red Rocks. Known as "Old Mrs. Johnson," she would allegedly pull a coat over her head and swing a hatchet to scare away her daughters' suitors. One of the trails at Red Rocks leads to an old graveyard where people think the woman may be buried. People have been known to stay in the graveyard at night to try to hear or see her. Other theories involve a homeless woman living in the area in the 1950s or a woman living in a cave, which has been fenced off to prevent people from exploring the area. This version of the story says the woman kills children that come too close to the cave and hides their bodies and severed limbs in the surrounding area. Supposedly, the ghost of the Hatchet Lady was upset when Hoyt began planning and building the area for the stage, and some say she may have interfered with construction as well.

The attire of a second Red Rocks ghost marks him as the specter of an old miner, and many people claim to have seen his apparition, which is clear enough that those who have can provide great detail about his appearance. He supposedly stands 5 feet 5 inches tall, has a long white beard, wears a brown hat, holds a bottle in his hand, and is mostly seen in the restricted areas of the stage. Outside of his appearance and seemingly unpleasant demeanor, not much is known about this ghost or why he haunts the area. His story does seem to lack the color of a blood-soaked headless woman wielding a bloody hatchet.

There have also been sightings of Indian spirits dressed in traditional ceremonial attire, and some of these sightings report the ghosts doing ceremonial dances.

One building in the park that has seen a lot of ghostly activity is the Trading Post, originally called the Indian Trading Post when it opened in 1931. The first caretaker actually lived in the basement, but it was later converted into a storage area. Inside it sold Indian wares that were provided by the Denver Art Museum. The current building still functions as a gift shop, with a small coffee café inside as well. The Denver Channel did a two-part story on the building in 2009 after several employees revealed their belief that the building was haunted.

The first consisted of interviews with staff about their experiences in the building and was called "Is Red Rocks Haunted?" In the story, several of the staff members said that they had gone down into the storage area to replenish products only to have boxes thrown at them when no one else was down there. One employee claimed that the voice of a man whispered her name in her ear, but when she turned to see who spoke, no one was there. Many of the employees also reported hearing footsteps. They also claimed a door would lock by itself and the handle would move when no one was around it. The door had a broken lock and handle when the story was written, because employees had to break in after the door supposedly locked itself. The tales continue, but the consensus among the employees is that they do not mind the presence of the ghosts in their workspace. They are even happy to tell customers that the building is haunted.

The second Denver Channel story invited the Rocky Mountain Paranormal Research Society to investigate the space, but the article is less about their findings and more about the organization itself. This is probably because they did not find anything after six hours at the site; they did not record any unusual audio, and their video cameras did not pick up anything unusual

either, according to their report of the investigation. In the previous article however, one employee decided that he would leave a
recording device in the Trading Post overnight and was able to
collect his own EVP. He recorded the sound of breathing, voices,
and moving boxes, noting that the room where he had made the
recordings had been empty all night.

Red Rocks Amphitheatre happens to be one of my all-time
favorite places in the world. While I cannot admit to personally
experiencing any ghostly activity there, I can say that there certainly is a magic about the place, and many people talk about the
spiritual feeling that is almost tangible at the site. The people of
Morrison must have felt the same way as the area was originally
called Garden of the Angels before the idea of the amphitheatre
came about. My recommendation is this: no matter how you feel
about ghosts, this should always be a stop when visiting Colorado.
You do not even need the excuse of a concert to go there, although
I highly recommend doing that too. If you decide to visit and nothing ghostly happens, the location is beautiful enough that it is
still worth the stop. If you like music, it is also nice to step into
the visitor center at the top of the amphitheatre. There is also a
short history of the venue that includes a Hall of Fame, as well as
a long wall on which every band that has ever played Red Rocks
is listed by year. There are also computers mounted on the walls
where visitors can watch videos of many of the shows. The Hall of
Fame also has concert paraphernalia from bands that have played
there and especially honors the Grateful Dead as the band that has
played the most concerts there.

CHAPTER 10

Hotel Boulderado
BOULDER

Opened in 1909, Hotel Boulderado has had many famous guests, reportedly including several ghosts.

IN THE EARLY 1900S, Boulder had begun to truly establish itself, and the gold that brought people there had made the city a successful mining town. Once the territory gained statehood, Boulder became the seat of a county of the same name. The city was home to a university (completed in 1877) and a railroad hub and had around 10,000 residents. The problem was it was not becoming the booming metropolis that municipal leaders had hoped it would.

So the Boulder City Council decided in a meeting that they needed a grand hotel to bring people in. While the city did have hotels, they decided that a more luxurious one was needed to accomplish their goals. Fundraising for the hotel was slow until one of the city leaders, who also happened to be the editor of Boulder's newspaper, the *Daily Camera*, decided to advertise their cause. He spread the idea through editorial, and it caught on in the city like wildfire, with shares being sold at $100 apiece to begin raising the funds for the hotel. By April 10, 1906, after only a few months of fundraising, the city had put together more than $80,000 and at one point was receiving contributions of up to $1,000 per day. Later that month, the Boulder Hotel Company was formed.

With the city residents wholeheartedly backing construction of the hotel, the city decided to let them decide on its design. Advertisements were placed in the paper asking architects to design one version of the building based on available funds and a second version of what they wanted to build if money were not a factor. William Redding & Son was the winning architectural company and investors then voted on which design they preferred, being allotted one vote per share purchased. The investors picked the second design. It would have five stories and would be the tallest building in Boulder at the time. The city had raised enough money by October to begin construction.

Despite the city's approval of the hotel, there was one setback: deciding on a name. Many thought that the hotel should be named after one of the pioneers who helped raise Boulder from the small town to the bustling mining city it was becoming. One of those pioneers, William R. Rathvon, had a different idea, and proposed naming it the Hotel Boulderado, combining the city's name with Colorado. Letters to the editor of the *Daily Camera* arrived in droves protesting the name as unoriginal and boring, however, and people were worried that the name would not stand the test of time. They wanted something that would still sound classy and new 20 years into the future of the hotel. Supporters of the name, on the other hand, challenged their opponents to come up with something better, and as no other name was proposed, Hotel Boulderado became the official title. More than 100 years later, the name still seems to work just fine.

Boulder raised an additional $75,000 to furnish the hotel. However, furniture did not arrive in time for their planned Thanksgiving opening in 1908 and instead the hotel opened its doors to guests on New Year's Day 1909. Rathvon and his wife were the first couple to sign the register. The hotel had 75 guest rooms, none of which ended in the number 13. The roof of the lobby reached up the second level and was an intricately designed stained glass canopy. The opening of the hotel sparked construction of other buildings throughout the city, such as an opera house, and residents of Boulder began to consider it the "Athens of the West."

When it first opened, a room in the Boulderado cost guests between $1 and $2.50, not including meals. It could cost more toward $50 if the guest planned on staying a full month, a price that included baths and meals. Many of the rooms had telephones and each had steam radiators and hot water.

After World War I, the hotel was the headquarters of a murder investigation for a short time. A police officer was shot while walking to work, and some thought he was killed because he knew locations of gambling rings and bootlegging operations. At one point the police chief was arrested on suspicion of hiring a hit man to kill the officer but was released due to a lack of evidence. After World War II, the hotel underwent renovations to modernize it, such as adding electric wiring and appliances. A second wing was also built, allowing the hotel to serve guests in 160 rooms. The hotel is very proud of its heritage and displays lots of antiques and other items from Boulder's history.

In 1959, the stained glass roof of the lobby was damaged by heavy snowfall, and it could not be repaired. A new roof was designed and installed in 1977, although it was not the same beautiful stained glass of the original and was instead made of plexiglass. The ceiling was later renovated in 2004, bringing back the stained glass. This renovation cost the hotel $65,000. From the lobby to the dining room, however, there is tile flooring that has been in the hotel since its grand opening and has welcomed guests to the Boulderado for more than 100 years. Another original item is an old-fashioned elevator that has to be operated by a hotel employee to this day.

When the hotel originally opened, Boulder was a dry county and would be until 1967, when the ban on liquor was repealed. Two years later, the hotel had remodeled its basement to open the Catacomb Bar (now called License No. 1). It was the first organization in the city to obtain a liquor license after the law was repealed.

Like many old hotels, the Boulderado is thought to be home to a number of spirits of a different kind, and many staff members have had paranormal experiences in the building. Many of the stories center around rooms 302 and 304, which are next to each other. When guests complain to the front desk about haunted activity, these rooms are the culprits most of the time. The rooms have a connecting door that makes them a popular option for some guests, and room 302 has a porch, again making it a desirable room.

Many haunted-tour guides and employees think that paranormal activity in this particular room is caused by an attempted double suicide (although I have not seen any record of this story). According to the story, a man killed himself on the bed using chloroform while his wife was taking a bath. When the woman entered the room and found her husband dead, she attempted to take the rest of the chloroform herself, but there was not enough left for a fatal dose. There are also some who say the room has hosted "multiple suicides" over the years, another one supposedly being a death by self-inflicted gunshot, but this tale is not as widely told as the one of the chloroform suicide.

Reports of activity in the adjoining suites claim that the lights and televisions will turn on by themselves. The old grandfather clock in the room has also been known to act strangely from time to time, and it will wildly spin its hands before landing on the correct time. According to the Boulder County Paranormal Research Society, a staff member was taking an American Indian guest to room 304, the only room available that night, and that visitor would not even touch the door. That person claimed to feel a spiritual presence in the room and left to stay at a different hotel, even though it was very early in the morning. Because of all this, the hotel has been known to keep the rooms open to the public on occasion for ghost tours.

One of the other spirits believed to cause activity in the building is a woman in a white dress who has been seen walking around the hotel's hallways. Kitchen items have been known to move around for no reason. Sometimes windows and doors will open on their own, despite being locked. One staff member said that while staying in room 306, he woke feeling like something was holding him to the bed and could not get up. There are also unexplained scratching sounds on the walls.

Boulder has long attracted visitors looking for a mountain getaway in Colorado. The city lies at the foot of the Rocky Mountains, is a short drive from several skiing hot spots, and is right in the middle of a drive from Denver to Estes Park. Paranormal enthusiasts looking to hit as many haunted locations as possible (and still make it to the Stanley Hotel) can use this as an in-between location for their route.

Boulder Theater

Since 1906, the Boulder Theater has been bringing people together with music in one way or another. In addition to the events and concerts held there year-round, the theater is also home to a seemingly well-loved paranormal resident known as George.

What is now the Boulder Theater was once the Curran Opera House, which first opened in 1906. In addition to opera performances, the theater also presented both musical productions and silent movies. *The Jazz Singer*, the first movie with talking, was released in 1927 by Warner Brothers and screened there. Like many theaters in the olden days, the Curran would present double features. During the Great Depression, it would give away bags of groceries to whomever was sitting in the lucky seat of the day.

In 1935, the Curran was purchased by the Fox Theater Company and was renamed the Boulder Theater. It was refurbished, expanded, and then reopened in January 1936. In 1981, more renovations were done to transform the theater into a concert venue, and it operated in this form for 15 months. However, the company had kept the original theater seating when it changed over to a music venue, and this greatly restricted the way the theater could run concerts. It closed in 1983. A new company called Livingston and Edwards acquired the theater in 1988 and once again renovated it into a multiuse theater; despite yet another change of hands, the theater continued to run in this fashion until 1993. In 1994 it was once again repurchased and reopened in 1995 with a special screening of the Marilyn Monroe film *Some Like It Hot*. The theater now hosts nearly 250 events annually, including concerts, film festivals, film screenings, and community events.

Next door to the theater is George's, a local café that combines food and local beers. It also may have attracted the Boulder Theater's resident ghost, George Paper. Originally, George's opened as the Lounge in June 2008, but after it did, Paper's ghost allegedly began to act out more than usual. Paper was the manager of the Boulder Theater in the 1920s, while it was still called the Curran Opera House. One day while attempting to fix a lighting rig, he slipped and fell into the wiring, accidentally hanging himself. Many people have described a figure matching Paper's appearance in the building, especially near the bathrooms and the projection room, where Paper is believed to have resided while working at the theater.

Paper's ghost allegedly scared an intruder who broke into the theater but was later found by the police hiding in the projection booth. The man said he kept seeing an old man wearing a hat in the building, but his description did not fit that of the manager, who was living there at the time, and resembled Paper instead. The same ghostly figure has been seen by employees walking into bathrooms as well, the door to the bathroom has been seen swinging by itself, and the faucets sometimes turn on and off on their own. Curiously, lightbulbs have also been removed from the backstage area, with no explanation as to where they went.

The Boulder Genealogical Society has a burial record for a George W. Paper, who died on April 3, 1944, and a simple grave marker gives his year of birth as 1897. Without knowing more, however, it is hard to tell if it is the same George Paper as the one who supposedly died in the theater. An online article about the renaming of George's says that the *Daily Camera* ran an obituary for Paper in April 1944, but the newspaper's website does not have a digital archive going that far back. After a conversation with a staff member at the University of Colorado in Boulder's library, I found that it does not digitize its records back that far either. I emailed the archive department to see if it had a copy hidden away somewhere but had no luck.

While he supposedly still visits the theater in his own way, the ghost seems to have been appeased to some extent since the restaurant next door to the Boulder Theater was renamed George's after him.

CHAPTER 11

Stanley Hotel

ESTES PARK

As the most haunted location in Colorado, and one of the most haunted buildings in the country, the Stanley Hotel needs no introduction. The hotel gives haunted tours on a daily basis.

WHEN WRITING A BOOK ON HAUNTED LOCATIONS in the state of Colorado, the Stanley Hotel simply cannot be overlooked. It was ranked as one of the top most-haunted buildings in the United States by Denver's KUSA/9News in September 2014 and is widely regarded as the most haunted place in Colorado. The hotel does not shy away from its haunted reputation and, in fact, thrives under the idea. Guests can even participate in haunted tours of the building and grounds with a tour guide named Scary Mary. It also hosts numerous horror film festivals throughout the year.

Another story that makes the hotel so popular involves Stephen King's *The Shining*. King was inspired to write this popular novel, which was published in 1977, after staying in the hotel. Later, in 1980, Stanley Kubrick was so enthralled by the novel that he made it into the popular movie of the same title. It is regarded as one of the best horror movies of all time, and the Stanley Hotel plays the film on loop, 24 hours a day, on channel 42. This movie, however, was not filmed on location at the Stanley Hotel because of a lack of necessary lighting and power, according to Kubrick. Supposedly King did not like Kubrick's film and felt that it ignored many of the themes in his book. According to tours at the hotel, King supervised a made-for-TV version of *The Shining* that was shot at the Stanley and aired in 1997. One of the more popular differences between the book and the movie is the giant hedge maze. King's version had giant hedge animals that moved and taunted characters, while Kubrick's movie had an eerie maze. In December 2014, the Stanley Hotel announced an international competition to design a maze, inspired by the idea in the film; the ribbon cutting for this new feature took place in June 2015.

Freelan Oscar Stanley came to Estes Park in 1903 after being diagnosed with tuberculosis. A year earlier he had started the Stanley Steamer Motor Carriage company in Massachusetts with his twin brother, Francis. The company built steam-engine cars, which were very popular for a time. The brothers also had a patent for dry plate photography that they would later sell to George Eastman (creator of Kodak). Stanley purchased 160 acres of land from a wealthy lord named Dunraven and founded the Estes Park Development Company with his business partner. Dunraven had come over from England and had attempted to buy nearly all the land in the city of Estes Park, but because he was not a US citizen he could not legally do so.

Once the land was purchased, Stanley and his partner began building the first of 11 buildings that would later comprise the hotel. The first one they built was the main building, for which they broke ground in 1907. The timber used in the construction

came from the hotel's neighbor, which is now the Rocky Mountain National Park. In 1900, there was a fire at Bear Lake in the
park, and much of the timber used in construction came from
that period. Some say that you can smell wood fires in the building on hot summer days because of this. Today, the hotel stands
on only 55 acres, although many of the original buildings are
still in use. However, the ice pond, water reservoir, and nine-
hole golf course have been replaced with grazing lands for local
wildlife, such as elk.

Stanley did more than just build the hotel. He knew that there
was no way to run a hotel without guests to stay in the rooms, so
he provided tourists with a way to reach the city via automobile by
building the first road from Lyons, Colorado, to Estes Park. Prior
to this, the only way of getting to the city was by train. He also
established water and power companies in Estes Park in 1908;
eventually built the first bank in the area; and helped to establish
Rocky Mountain National Park, the Estes Park Fairgrounds, and
Stanley Park.

The hotel opened its doors to guests in 1909. Each room
had a phone, running water, indoor toilets, and electricity. It
was heated by the large fireplaces on the main floor, although
heating was not a problem, as the hotel ran only in the summer
season until 1984; heat was added to rooms in 1979. Since its
opening, it has been renovated on multiple occasions to bring it
back to its full splendor. The hotel and surrounding village were
powered by a hydroelectric plant until 1982, when it was closed
due to a large flood.

In 2009, the hotel celebrated 100 years of wowing the nation
as a successful haunted hotel. No one is sure when the haunts
in question started. Several different apparitions and instances
of paranormal activity have been reported throughout the building, especially in the lobby. Stanley himself, as one might expect,
has ostensibly been seen throughout the building. Additionally,

his wife, Flora, who was a professional pianist, is thought to be the unseen player that tickles the keys later at night in the Music Room (although some report that it is not Flora but her husband who plays the ghostly tunes).

The fourth floor of the hotel is another location where paranormal activity is often reported. Dunraven, the wealthy man from whom Stanley bought the land, is reportedly seen in room 407, accompanied by the smell of his tobacco pipe. It is strange that Dunraven's ghost should appear here, however, as he never stayed in the hotel and had left the country before it was even built. The lights also seem to have a mind of their own in the room, and there have been reports of a ghostly face looking out the window when the room is not occupied. According to an online video tour of the hotel led by Scary Mary, the fourth floor was originally a cavernous attic and was one of the few locations where children were permitted. People have said they can hear the sound of children laughing and running through the halls, especially in room 418. Some have reported the sound of bouncing balls, and others still have reported the feeling of being tucked in at night, a duty given to the children's nannies. There is a closet that notoriously opens and closes on its own in room 401, and in room 428 people report hearing footsteps on the roof and their furniture being moved around. There is also a reportedly friendly ghost called the Cowboy in that room, whose apparition tends to stand near one of the corners of the foot of the bed.

In December 1970, one of the housekeepers was cleaning the dance floor area in the MacGregor Ballroom when she found herself part of a ghostly party with guests in period clothing. She left to ask the front desk if anyone else had seen anything, and upon her return found the party still going. There are also reports of hearing footsteps when no one is there, as well as elevators operating on their own. In short, almost every room at the hotel has a paranormal complaint of some sort: human-shaped indentations in the bed, furniture moving on its own, and the list continues. And even though children were allowed only on the fourth floor, there are reports of a small child calling for his nanny on the second floor. Allegedly, it has been seen by several people, even King himself.

Perhaps one of the most popular ghost stories associated with the building is that of Elizabeth Wilson, who was chief housekeeper during some the hotel's first years of operation. On June 25, 1911, there was an explosion in the hotel during a storm while Wilson was lighting acetylene lanterns, the hotel's backup lighting. There had been an unknown gas leak in the room, and the flame Wilson was using to light the lanterns caused a combustion fire, according to a story by the *Estes Park Trail Gazette* in early 2014. The article quotes the hotel's archivist as saying that the explosion damaged 10% of the hotel's overall area and that the fire luckily put itself out, as it otherwise could have burned the whole building down. It caused Wilson to be shot from room 217 into the MacGregor Dining Room below it, where she survived with two broken ankles. All records from that period of the hotel's history are gone, however, and the same archivist cited in the article said there is no record of an Elizabeth Wilson, and every newspaper in the state published its own version of the explosion story. But, as the article continues, in 2014 evidence of the explosion was discovered, when bits of drywall covered by wallpaper that was in room 217 at the time of the explosion were found in an employee tunnel.

Since the '50s, allegedly after Wilson's death, guests staying in room 217 have reported additional levels of care and housekeeping, such as finding their items packed or unpacked for them. This was the room King stayed in when he became inspired to write *The Shining* in 1974, the night before the hotel shut down for the winter. King and his wife were the only guests in the building at the time. A claw-footed bathtub can be found in the room, recalling the famous scene in Kubrick's film, in which Jack Nicholson walks into a seemingly deserted room to find a beautiful woman in an old-fashioned tub. The room also contains a library of King's novels, including *The Shining*, of course, and any guests not feeling the spooky vibes of the hotel can always curl up with one of the books to put them in the mood.

As mentioned earlier, the hotel does not shy away from its reputation as the most haunted hotel in Colorado. As a matter of fact, in addition to daily historical tours, the hotel also gives daily haunted tours. Its website lists several tour packages, including a historical/paranormal combo tour, a nighttime ghost tour, and a five-hour ghosthunt through the most haunted areas of the hotel. All of the tours require advance booking and have separate costs. According to the article in the *Estes Park Trail Gazette,* the Stanley earns more than $1 million on tours alone. It also has a "haunted photo gallery" that includes spoof ghost photos of different locations in the hotel. Its online store includes items that pay homage to *The Shining* with oozing, bloodlike lettering spelling out "REDRUM." There is even an annual horror film festival there, dubbed the Stanley Film Festival, that was founded in 2013 by the Stanley Hotel.

Of all of the haunted locations I chose for this book, the Stanley Hotel had the most feedback about it from the people I knew, and it seems like everyone I talked to had a story to tell. My father, who usually loves a good scare, insisted that the hotel is not haunted and that it pays people to rattle guests' doors at night. On the other hand, some of the other people I talked to said they had trouble sleeping there because they felt like they were being watched. One guest said she saw the silhouette of a person standing outside the sliding shower doors while she was taking a shower. Numerous celebrities have stayed in the hotel as well, such as Jim Carrey, who stayed there during the filming of *Dumb and Dumber*. Allegedly, Carrey asked for the scariest room—he was placed in room 217—and was unable to finish the night there. Rumors around the hotel were that he could not make it three hours in the room, but he apparently never told anyone of his experiences.

Photos taken of the hotel have been known to depict orbs or even ghostly silhouettes. One area of the hotel, a stairwell, creates a sort of vortex of activity in images, and photos of that area often show greenish orbs. Sometimes, the more human-shaped ghosts that appear in photos are seen in rooms or areas where guests are not allowed or are not staying in at the time. For example, the tower area is closed to guests and has been for several years, but photographers who have taken pictures of events like weddings at the hotel have been known to call the front desk claiming to see people in their photos of the tower.

Interestingly enough, if you ask employees why they believe the hotel is haunted, some will say there are large deposits of quartz magnetite and limestone underneath the site that help channel spiritual energy into the building. Supposedly, this is why it is such a hot spot for ghostly activity, and employees have been recorded saying this on numerous ghosthunting television shows. Members of the *Ghost Hunters* show also claimed their research led them to believe that the mineral deposits were what caused the residual hauntings (i.e., snapshots of past events that continuously repeat themselves).

Perhaps predictably, the scientific minds at the Rocky Mountain Paranormal Research Society (RMPRS) had a bone to pick with this theory. They have come to the Stanley on numerous investigations, and Bryan Bonner, one of its founding members, was even there during the filming of King's version of *The Shining* (he was photographing a wedding). In all their research, however, they never came across any information about what was underneath it. To determine what was beneath the hotel, they contacted the Department of Agriculture, which has information on soils. It turns out that the property the Stanley is on had never been tested, so the society obtained permission to help participate in the first soil samplings. According to Bonner, four government agencies participated and performed ground-penetrating radar surveys, physical digs, and even something called an electromagnetic induction. RMPRS was included as a participant in an official government report stating that there is nothing but dirt beneath the hotel, and the report, details of the investigation, and pictures from it can all be seen on the group's website. After the survey of the soil was complete, RMPRS presented its findings to both staff at the hotel and *Ghost Hunters*. The next year, however, a different ghosthunting TV series came to see the Stanley, and hotel staff members were still telling people that they believe the paranormal activity was caused by mineral deposits under the hotel, despite the information given to them by the society.

Much of the hotel's fame is due to the success of King's book and Kubrick's film. Are the ghosts just there to play along, or is the Stanley Hotel really as haunted as they say? The best way to find out is to visit it yourself. Say hi to Ms. Wilson for me when you do.

East

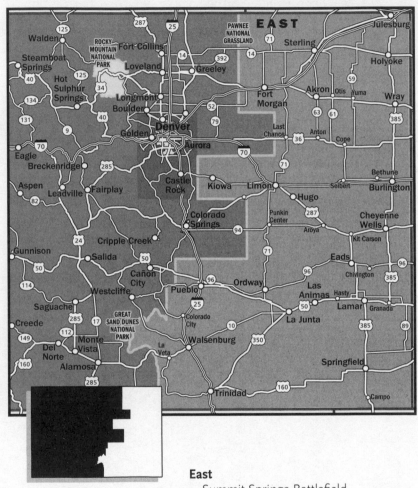

East
Summit Springs Battlefield
Sand Creek Massacre

CHAPTER 12

Summit Springs Battlefield
OTIS

This marker recognizes a 15-year-old boy who was killed trying to warn the tribes that an attack was coming, saving the lives of many people.

WHILE COLORADO IS FULL OF alleged paranormal activity and ghost sightings, there are also many literal ghost towns. Summit Springs existed in the early days of Colorado but did not last into the present, instead becoming one of dozens of villages, mining towns, and other small cities whose high hopes were not realized.

Perhaps what helped to bring about the downfall of Summit Springs was a battle that happened there on July 11, 1869. It was another tragic example of the strife between the American Indians that lived in Colorado and the military forces attempting to keep them from raiding the settlers. This particular attack came from the U.S. Army's 5th Cavalry Regiment, which included 244 soldiers and officers, along with 50 Pawnee scouts. This unit was led by Col. Eugene A. Carr, and one of his men was William "Buffalo Bill" Cody, who would later reenact the battle in his world-famous Wild West show. The attack was against a group of Cheyenne warriors called the Dog Soldiers, who had a violent reputation and were led by Chief Tall Bull.

This battle was a result of years of back-and-forth conflict between the Cheyenne in the area and new groups settling in the state of Kansas. Colorado was still a territory at the time and would not gain statehood until 1876, but the battles began spilling over into its eastern sections. In May 1869, men of the 5th Cavalry from Fort Lyon, Colorado, were heading toward Nebraska. Between then and the attack on July 11, there were several incidents between the white soldiers and Indian tribes, with casualties on both sides. However, once the cavalrymen used up their rations, they continued on to Fort McPherson, Nebraska. Once they were gone Chief Tall Bull proceeded to attack in several locations in Kansas, including a Danish settlement. Jeff Broome, author of *Libbie Custer's Encounter with Tom Alderdice . . . The Rest of the Story*, called the 1860s the most violent decade in Kansas history, and episodes like this contributed to that.

Susanna Alderdice, who was captured during the Cheyenne raids along with another woman, was the only American casualty during the Summit Springs Battle. When she was kidnapped, she was staying with another family, and its members managed to safely escape. However, historians agree that Susanna may have been slower to get away from the Indian horsemen because she had three sons and an 8-month-old daughter with her. Her three sons were beaten, killing two of them, and her daughter Alice was taken captive along with Susanna herself. She was taken from an area in Lincoln County, Kansas, a settlement nearly 30 miles west of Salina, Kansas.

Allegedly, her husband, Tom, began following the trail of the captors after discovering the bodies of the two boys, his son and stepson. The third boy, Willis, also a stepson, was seriously wounded but still alive when Tom returned to the settlement. In addition to several other wounds, it was recorded that Willis had an arrow in his back that had sunk a full 5 inches into his body. He was 4 years old at the time, and the wound would cause him to walk with a limp for the rest of his life. Tom had not been at the house at the time of the raid, as he was going for supplies with other settlers in Salina. Once he found the trail of the Dog Soldiers, he was hoping to get into contact with Army soldiers in the hopes of rescuing his wife. He eventually gave a description of his wife to Lt. Col. George Armstrong Custer at Fort Leavenworth but continued to search on his own. At Fort Leavenworth he was also interviewed by two newspapers about his wife's kidnapping.

Once Tom had resumed his own search for the Dog Soldiers, the trail led to his daughter, Alice, whom he found dead. His wife had not been able to continue carrying her, and the Cheyenne killed her three days after capturing them, according to Broome, who compiled a history of the event from the diaries of Custer's wife, Elizabeth "Libbie" Custer. It is suspected that the small child made lots of noise and would have been difficult to care for as a captive, which might have led to her murder.

On June 9, 1869, the command was given for the 5th Cavalry to clear the Republican River area in eastern Kansas of all Indians, which led to more fighting with Tall Bull's warriors. The Army began following the warriors in an attempt to prevent them from escaping into the Wyoming Territory. This is what brought both the cavalry and the Dog Soldiers into the Colorado Territory. Col. Carr was able to camp in an unseen location, which aided his surprise attack on the tribes. He also cut his number of soldiers to the 244 present in the battle to help his troops move more swiftly. This culminated in the Battle of Summit Springs. While one of the goals was to force the tribes out of the Kansas area, another was to safely rescue Susanna and the other female captive. It is said that Summit Springs was the decisive battle between the Plains tribes of Colorado and the government here, ending the conflict between the two. Part of this was because the remaining Dog Soldiers split into two factions, one group going to join the Cheyenne in the north, and the other the Cheyenne in the south.

At the time of the battle, 84 lodges housed approximately 450 members of the Cheyenne tribe in the area. There were women and children there, along with the white women being held captive. Fighting started in the middle of the afternoon and caught the Indians completely by surprise. It lasted only three hours, but more than 50 Indians were killed, including Tall Ball and several women and children, among them Susanna. Only one U.S. Army soldier was wounded. Alderdice was 29 and pregnant with her fifth child at the time of her death; she was buried the next day in an unmarked grave on the battlefield. Carr initially wanted to name the area Susanna Springs but could not once he found out the area was already called Summit Springs. After the battle, all of the lodges were burned and everything was destroyed, including food, clothing, and weapons. Nothing was left untouched. Seventeen Indian women, one of them Tall Bull's wife, were taken captive, along with all the horses and mules.

There are at least four markers in the Summit Springs Battlefield area. One is a monument erected in 1934 that commemorates the battle, as well as Tall Bull and Susanna's deaths. It also recognizes the second captive, who was wounded in the battle but lived. Later, in 1970, the great-grandson of Tall Bull placed a second monument at the location, saying he prayed that all men "live in harmony and respect one another." His plaque recognized the individual Indian warriors who were killed, as well as the 15-year-old herd boy who died helping his people escape the battlefield. A third marker is harder to find, as it

Terrain on the eastern side of Colorado is vastly different from that of its mountainous west. There might be some slight rolling hills, such as this one next to the Summit Springs Battlefield, but for the most part, the land is flat enough that, on a clear day, visitors can see for miles all around.

lies flat on the ground; it marks where Tall Bull's tepee stood. Yet another marker, which is also very difficult to find, marks the spot where soldiers found Susanna dying. Even though her grave is unmarked, the marker says that she was buried on the hill overlooking the area.

With such a violent history, it is no surprise that there could be spirits lingering around this battlefield, and it is rumored that the area is haunted by the Indians who died there. Many visitors have said that despite the battlefield's location in a windy area of the plains, it is eerily quiet near the actual site, a stillness that makes it easy to imagine the sounds and feel of the battle that took place there. Who is it that haunts the battlefield? Whether it is the restless spirits of the Indians who died in the battle, the ghost of Susanna forever remembering the misery of the last three weeks of her life, or both, is unclear. Either way, the area continues to have a daunting aura.

CHAPTER 13

Sand Creek Massacre

CHIVINGTON

These boards feature copies of letters written by the two American soldiers who held their group of men back during the massacre. They wrote the letters to a superior officer condemning the actions of the attack's leader, Col. Jack. M. Chivington. Most of the American Indians who died in the attack were women, children, and elderly people.

BEFORE COLORADO BECAME A STATE or was even thought of by the American people, it was home to several American Indian tribes. Throughout its early history, the pioneers and miners who came to the area began taking the land from these tribes. Later, deals and treaties were enacted to enable the tribes to keep their land, but these were often never honored. Some of the tribe members also disobeyed these treaties and continued to roam where they wished. Two tribes were located near modern-day Eads, Colorado, very close to the border of

Kansas, and some members of the Cheyenne and Arapahoe tribes had settled in the area and created a village.

Land the two tribes had settled in was protected by the Treaty of Fort Laramie, signed by the United States and seven native tribes in 1851, including the Cheyenne and Arapahoe. The land included southeast Wyoming, southwestern Nebraska, most of eastern Colorado, and western Kansas. In 1858, however, the Pikes Peak gold rush caused hundreds of people to rush into Colorado and later Kansas. In 1861, a new treaty was signed by six southern Cheyenne chiefs and four Arapahoe chiefs. The Treaty of Fort Wise took away most of the land given to the tribes in the Fort Laramie treaty. In fact, their new reserve in eastern Colorado was less than one-thirteenth the size of their original land.

Due to the small size of their new home, food became scarce for the tribes. Many of them would leave their reservation to hunt for game, which led to their allegedly killing the livestock of the new settlers or taking their possessions. Newspapers began writing stories about the dangers of attacks by Indians on the white settlers. Some of the attacked settlers were killed, and the murders of one family in particular caused many settlers to want revenge. In response to these acts, John Evans, the territorial governor at the time, created the Colorado 3rd Regiment in August 1864 and put his friend, Methodist preacher John M. Chivington, in charge of its soldiers. The US government could not spare soldiers because of the ongoing Civil War but allowed Evans to recruit his own men. Around 1,000 volunteers, few of which had military training, signed up for 100 days of service, the government-approved period of service. The job came with a promotion to Colonel for Chivington, who had previously made a small name for himself defeating Texans who had planned on invading Colorado via New Mexico during the Civil War. This is, unfortunately, not the legacy for which he is now remembered.

Evans had asked that all tribes report to Fort Lyons to be considered peaceful and said that any who did not come would be considered hostile. Many did not respond to this ultimatum and it has been postulated that, due to the short notice and the distance between tribes, some of them never even received the notices. Chief Black Kettle of the Cheyenne responded in late August, and a meeting with him was later held to negotiate peace terms. Other chiefs would later follow his example. These peace talks, however, would not last long. The original, more understanding commander at Fort Lyons was quickly replaced by one who did not want the fort's resources to go toward feeding the Indian refugees. He told them to leave and that they could safely camp on the banks of Big Sandy Creek, an area often mistakenly called Sand Creek. He gave them back their weapons and told them to use them to hunt for themselves, as he could no longer afford to feed them. Many witnesses also stated that he gave Black Kettle the white flag of peace before leaving.

Once Chivington learned there was a group of Arapahoe who were under Chief Left Hand and a group of Cheyenne under Black Kettle camping for the winter near Big Sandy Creek, he resolved to attack them. The man who gave him the tribe's whereabouts was the very officer who turned the tribes away from Fort Lyons and, in fact, he reported to Chivington that they were hostile. Before dawn on November 29, 1864, Chivington and his approximately 700 troops approached the Indian camp.

"I don't tell you to kill all ages and sexes, but look back on the Plains of the Platte, where your mothers, fathers, brothers, sisters have been slain," Chivington told his men. Proceeding with their attack, the soldiers caught the approximately 500 Indians camping in their lodges by surprise. It is estimated that only 130 of the people in camp at the time were warriors, as the rest of the men were out hunting. What Chivington did not know before the battle was that a smaller group of men, which included a John Smith

This monument commemorates the site of the massacre, in what was at the time the Colorado Territory.

and Pvt. David Louderback, had already been sent to the camp to find out if the camping tribes were friendly. They had also brought another man along to help them trade with the Indians.

Chivington moved quickly, sending groups of men to cut the tribes off from their horses. Thinking the attack was a mistake, Black Kettle of the Cheyenne tribe raised both an American and a white flag showing that his people were there in peace. Some records state that another chief from the Cheyenne, a man in his 70s named White Antelope, ran forward asking the troops not to shoot and eventually folded his arms over his chest to indicate that the tribes had no intentions of fighting. Knowing he would die, he sang a death song, according to witnesses, as he stood with arms crossed and was shot while doing so. Smith quickly realized what was going on and also attempted to wave a white flag but was not recognized and was shot at by the soldiers.

Louderback also attempted to stop the fighting, but Chivington paused the battle only long enough for him and the other men to move to the rear of the attacking soldiers.

It is important to note Chivington's chilling preattack instructions as it is estimated that nearly 163 Indians were killed that day, almost all of them women, children, and elderly people. Some of the women were also raped, and many of the bodies were scalped or mutilated. Nine of Chivington's men were killed and 28 were wounded in the melee. Allegedly, Chivington saw both of the chiefs' attempts to bring peace and intentionally ignored their pleas. The savage attack was over by 3 p.m., but there are suggestions that some of the soldiers looted the bodies after the fighting, taking everything from jewelry to body parts, and that Chivington made no attempts to stop them. While some of the Indians managed to escape, they were pursued by soldiers, and any that remained at the camp were killed, as Chivington did not want to take prisoners.

In his report, Chivington listed that both White Antelope and Black Kettle were killed. Some historians say that Left Hand was also killed, but others say he escaped. Additionally, Black Kettle would sign a treaty in 1865, showing that he escaped as well. He was able to rescue his wife, but both were killed in a different attack years later. Discrepancies in who was killed and who escaped are also muddled by Chivington's fluffing of numbers. Historians agree that in his military report, a letter describing a "glorious battle" to the *Rocky Mountain News*, as well as in his own testimony later on, the number of Indian deaths he reported was much higher than the total number killed.

Controversy surrounded the attack. At first, Chivington was praised as a hero, and people began calling it the Battle of Sand Creek. Others, however, did not see it that way. In fact, some of Chivington's men, such as Capt. Silas M. Soule, commanded his men not to partake in the battle, as the Indians had been given permission to camp there. Eventually, Congress's attention was called away from the Civil War to investigate Chivington's actions. The event was studied and testimony from both sides was given. Soule was asked to testify but was mysteriously shot before he could. Smith would testify against Chivington, and one of his statements included rough visuals on the depth of mutilation to the dead bodies of the Cheyenne and Arapahoe people. Washington decided it was not a battle but a massacre, and both Evans and Chivington were forced to resign their posts, but that was the only punishment they received for their actions. While it is now most commonly known as the Sand Creek Massacre, there are some who call it simply the Chivington Massacre, plainly laying blame on the man they hold responsible for the lives taken that day.

Close to one year after the attack, people began reporting Indian campsites near the site of the massacre, but when the reports were investigated, no trace of a camp was found. Most reported an eerie stillness about the ghost camp, as if the people were frozen in time. Attempts were made in 1911 to photograph the camp, although none were successful. Later, when others saw the camp and tried to investigate, it would disappear in the mist, leaving only the cry of a mourning woman behind. Other reports include seeing spirits of Indians looking "accusingly" at those passing by the massacre site. There are the sounds of children crying when no one is around, as well as the sounds of chanting, dogs barking, and children screaming. People around the area of the massacre have reported feeling extreme pain and anguish, and one group of archaeologists also reported members of its team needing to leave, as they felt overwhelming sadness and grief as they excavated the site. Spirits are most often seen there on November 29, but it's unclear whether they are a moment of emotional turmoil frozen in time or simply specters reminding us of a black spot in Colorado's history.

South Central

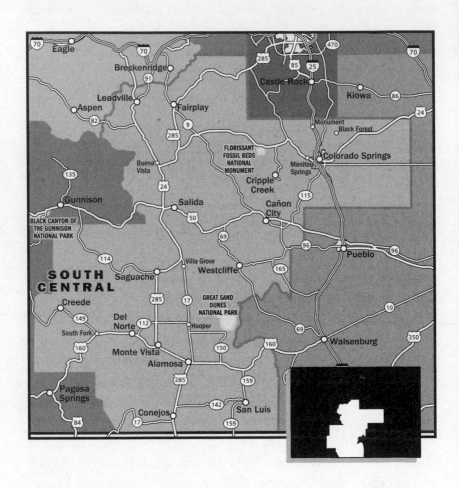

South Central
Bloody Espinosa Brothers
Broadmoor
Cave of the Winds

Crawford Family
Miramont Castle
Museum of Colorado Prisons

CHAPTER 14

Bloody Espinosa Brothers
Various Locations

The Espinosa brothers are thought to be two of the country's first serial killers. While their victims were all found in the southern area of Colorado, some believe they haunt parts of the capitol building in Denver.

THE STORY OF AMERICA'S FIRST SERIAL KILLERS, the Bloody Espinosa Brothers, starts not in Colorado but south of it, and their ghosts may haunt a couple of different places within the state. There is debate about exactly where the Espinosas were born. Some place their birth in the New Mexico Territory, while others say they may have been born in Vera Cruz, Mexico. There is also some confusion as to what caused these men to become such violent murderers and debate about what started their vendetta. Some accounts say that they were part of a bad land trade and later tax revolt against the Americans after the Mexican–American War.

In James E. Perkins's book *Tom Tobin: Frontiersman*, he presents a version of the Espinosas' story that starts with their being part of a poor family in the city of El Rito, 35 miles west of Taos, New Mexico. Unlike many other children in the area, the Espinosa siblings could read and write and were presumably taught to do so by local priests.

Felipe Espinosa was 19 when what became known as the Taos Revolt took place, and there is no evidence that anyone from the El Rito area took part in the fighting. Although New Mexico was a territory of the United States at the time, many Mexican American citizens were still loyal to the Mexican government and did not appreciate US troops controlling their cities. Revolts started in Santa Fe and spread to Taos, where fighting began in January 1847. Once the uprising had largely been suppressed, many citizens of Taos were arrested and charged throughout March and April of 1847 and, as they had previously been granted US citizenship, could be tried in the US court system. Twenty-eight of them were hanged for participating in the revolt (although this did not kill the rebellion entirely and outbreaks of violence continued for several months). It is suggested that Felipe may have known several of the people hanged by the American troops and that this helped spark his hatred of the Anglos.

In 1854 Felipe decided to marry—and what better way to find a bride than by kidnapping two women from a neighboring city? He had to journey to another community, as many people in El Rito felt that something was wrong with Felipe, and the fathers there would not permit him to court their daughters. Felipe married Maria Secundina Hurtado of Santa Ana after abducting her and one of her sisters, and they would eventually have three children together. They lived near her parents for a short time, until they relocated to San Rafael, Colorado. By then, the remaining members of Felipe's family had also relocated there from El Rito, and his wife's family joined them in Colorado as well. The Espinosas lived in a small, one-room house until Felipe and his brother Vivian, could afford to build and add other rooms. The Hurtados built a similar one-room house next door. Felipe and Vivian would later help construct a church in San Rafael.

It was Felipe's decision to begin stealing horses, and thereafter to rob freight wagons, that launched the brothers on their murderous rampage. However, in 1863 one of the wagon drivers they stole from recognized the brothers and was able to tell authorities where they lived. Although the Espinosa brothers were able to escape, the soldiers stole almost all of the household items from their families, along with some of their livestock, as punishment for helping the brothers escape. The soldiers would later report that they took only what they thought the brothers had stolen. With their family now facing starvation, Felipe took his brother northeast on March 10, 1863, and the two began to kill any Anglo men they could find for revenge.

There is another, more widely recounted theory for the Espinosas' actions that plays more on Felipe's zealous religious nature. Both he and his brother were members of Los Hermanos Penitentes, a group of men who were known for atoning for their sins with flagellation, both of themselves and others. In fact, when Felipe's wife was first kidnapped, she escaped home and showed her family the marks from where Felipe had whipped her. The Penitentes were also known to drag heavy crosses and bind their limbs to prevent blood circulation as a way of cleansing themselves of sin. Up until 1890, they were a public religious group prevalent in Colorado and New Mexico, and their subsequent secrecy is due to a letter written in 1886 by the Archbishop of Santa Fe asking them to stop flagellation. This religious sect, however, was very active in the Espinosas' time, and Felipe was particularly devout.

It is said that six of his relatives were killed during the violence in their area, and that some of the women were raped, although there is scant evidence for any of this. People began to claim that Felipe received a vision from the Virgin Mary, who said for every member of the Espinosa family killed he must kill 100 Anglos. And so, the brothers' rampage began.

In May 1863, they found their first victim in Fremont County, near the area of California Gulch, viciously mutilating his corpse and hacking the heart out of his chest. There was a note attached that read, "Vengeance was to be reaped upon the Americans as a sacrifice to the Virgin."

John Evans, who was the governor of the territory at the time, allegedly received a letter from Felipe that said he would kill 600 gringos unless he and his kin received pardons for their crimes, as well as 5,000 acres of land in Conejos County. Felipe pushed the matter further by stating the governor would be one of the 600 killed if his demands were not met. By this time, the Espinosas had killed several people in a manner similar to that of their first victim, shooting some, stabbing others, and violently mutilating several of them after their deaths. One victim had a small cross carved into his chest. One of the victims, Henry Harkins, was killed on March 18, 1863, near present day Cañon City, and shortly after his death the area in which he was found became known as Dead Man's Canyon.

After several people from California Gulch had been killed, some of the people from the area tracked down Felipe and Vivian and ambushed them 3 miles from the city of Fairplay. One got a clean shot at an unsuspecting Vivian and hit him in the ribs from behind as he was preparing the horses for the Espinosas to leave camp. After a short gunfight, Felipe was able to escape, but

Vivian was killed and left where he fell. Felipe escaped back to San Rafael and laid low until nagging guilt forced him to return to learn his brother's fate. He later buried Vivian and returned to San Rafael to recruit his 16-year-old nephew, Jose, to finish his and Vivian's unfinished work.

In response to the supposed letter, Governor Evans put a $1,500 bounty on each of the Espinosas' heads. Tom Tobin, a mountain man and tracker who was distantly related to the them by marriage, was contracted by the military to help track them down. Tobin and a small group of soldiers found them near a campsite, where the tracker shot and killed both of them, gunning down Jose as he attempted to escape. Tobin and his companions decided that to prove what they had accomplished and claim the bounties, they would take the heads back to Evans in Denver, leaving the decapitated bodies unburied. Once they arrived in the capital, however, the governor did not fulfill his end of the deal and only paid a small portion of the bounty. Outraged citizens responded by pooling their money to buy Tobin a silver-plated rifle. It is estimated that the Espinosas killed at least 25 and as many as 32 people before being slain themselves.

The heads of the Espinosas were kept in jars in the tunnels underneath the capitol building, which had been converted for storage. The Rocky Mountain Paranormal Research Society claims that distant relatives of the Espinosas told them on one of the society's ghost tours that the skulls were later found and cremated at the capitol building. This was not the last of the Espinosas, however, and some people claim to have seen the decapitated heads of Felipe and Jose floating around the storage tunnels of the capitol. Some members of the cleaning staff claim they have seen these grisly specters as high up as the third floor of the building. There are also tour guides who claim people can hear the hoofbeats of the Espinosas' horses as they tried to make their escape.

Officials at the capitol building, however, strongly deny any paranormal activity there. There is also some confusion as to whom the heads belong to. The story is that it is the heads of the Espinosa brothers that float around the capitol, but Vivian was killed separately, months before Felipe. In fact, Perkins wrote in his book that Vivian's head was shot and blown apart in the gunfight. He also notes that Felipe took one of his brother's shriveled feet with him when he came back to bury the body. Of the three men, Felipe and his nephew Jose were the ones who were beheaded.

The bodies, on the other hand, are a different story. Vivian was killed and left unburied near their camp near Ute Pass until Felipe came back later to bury the skeletal remains. This pass is an important location for the Espinosas, as it is estimated that they killed 12 of their victims in the area. Some people claim to have seen the headless bodies of the brothers together in Ute Pass, and some say they have seen the apparition of one of them carrying what looks to be a lumpy head in his arms. Again, this story is attributed to the headless Espinosa brothers but may actually refer to Felipe and Jose. Many legends surrounding ghosts involve the idea that a spirit is not at rest if the body is not buried intact. In the case of the Espinosas, two members of the family may not have been properly buried at all, let alone with their heads—and, in Vivian's case, a foot.

CHAPTER 15

Broadmoor
COLORADO SPRINGS

A man-made lake, a golf course, and large condos surround the massive Broadmoor hotel.

IN THE CITY OF COLORADO SPRINGS there are two distinct areas. There is a normal downtown sort of area with restaurants, shops, and small surrounding residences. Then, as the city spreads upward on the mountainside, there is the area where the Broadmoor is located. This hotel is simply massive, with several buildings, a bowling alley, a two-floor piano bar, a lake, and a golf club. But to understand the grandeur of the Broadmoor, one must first understand Spencer Penrose.

Spencer came to Colorado Springs from Philadelphia in 1891 to visit his childhood friend Charles L. Tutt Sr. During his visit, rumors emerged that people were striking it rich and finding huge gold reserves in the nearby city of Cripple Creek. Both Tutt and Spencer sought their own riches near Pikes Peak, and the fortune Spencer would later receive was only the beginning of what would become his vast wealth.

Spencer decided to make Colorado Springs his permanent residence and spent his earnings on different transportation methods throughout the city, as well as on improving roads for automobiles. One of his stranger purchases was contracting the Will Rogers Shrine of the Sun in 1938, which overlooks the city of Colorado Springs from high up on Cheyenne Mountain. Its tower lights up at night and can be seen for miles; it honors comedian Will Rogers, whom Spencer admired and who had died in a plane crash shortly before construction began. This shrine, however, is now Spencer's final resting place, and the locals consider it to be more of a monument to him. In fact, it is said that he originally intended to name it for himself but was convinced otherwise.

One of Spencer's other popular projects is the Cheyenne Mountain Zoo, which is still open today. During the zoo's construction in 1926, Spencer's exotic animal collection stayed on the grounds of the Broadmoor, and he had collected around 200 creatures by the time of the zoo's opening. It is one of the more popular and successful privately owned menageries in the country and has the honor of being the zoo at the highest altitude in the country. In 1937 Spencer and his wife, Julie, also created the El Pomar foundation, which enabled the city's wealthy to donate money that the organization would then use to aid different charitable projects throughout the community. After Spencer's death, Julie continued with the organization as its president, and the foundation still gives $20 million annually in grants to the Colorado area.

The Will Rogers Shrine of the Sun overlooks the city of Colorado Springs from high up on Cheyenne Mountain and honors humorist Will Rogers. It is also the final resting place of builder Spencer Penrose.

Spencer is something of a legend in Colorado Springs, particularly in the Cheyenne Mountain area, and most residents are familiar with his history and the resulting tales associated with him. One particular legend is that when Spencer decided to become a hotel owner, he resolved to purchase the Antlers, but the owners refused to sell it to him for the $125,000 he offered. Spencer was very offended by this snub and vowed to own a hotel that would surpass the Antlers. Some say that this is why the letter *a* in the copyrighted logo of the Broadmoor is smaller but more conspicuous than the rest of the letters and that this was Spencer's way of saying he won. Some also speculate that the smaller *a* was a reminder of the poor treatment he received at the Antlers hotel after not being recognized by the staff. The Antlers hotel still exists in Colorado Springs and is now run by Hilton Hotels but remains quite in the shadow of the Broadmoor. The Broadmoor

The Broadmoor hotel in Colorado Springs has a reputation for class and luxury. It is supposedly haunted by Julie Penrose, the wife of the man who built the hotel.

also has a chain of banks in the city and has its own small shopping center, which has 26 retail shops for hotel guests.

In the late 1800s, land the hotel now sits on was originally the Broadmoor Dairy Farm, and its owner eventually started creating a system of roadways on the 2,400-acre plot. He had what was at first called Broadmoor Lake built on the property in 1889, and, to get people to buy his plots of land, he built a casino. It was completed in 1891, but it buried the owner in debt, and the month after it opened, he lost the farm. The casino kept running but it did not seem to prosper and was destroyed in a fire in

1897. The hotel that had recently been added next to it survived, however, and the gambling hall was later rebuilt.

After the Antlers refused his proposition, Spencer set his sights on the Broadmoor Hotel and Casino. By May 1916, he had purchased the land with the hotel and casino, which totaled 18 acres, plus an additional 400 acres of the surrounding land, all of which set him back $90,000. He had the casino moved and it would later become the golf club building. He decided to build his new hotel on the east side of Broadmoor Lake—now called Cheyenne Lake—and hired a firm from New York to design it in January 1917. He also acquired an additional 800–900 acres of land while the plans for the hotel were still being designed.

Both Spencer and Julie were deeply involved in the design and decoration of the hotel. Spencer's friend Charles Tutt Sr. died in 1909 and did not live to see the purchase of the hotel, but his son Charles L. Tutt Jr. continued to help the Penroses in its development. Even after Spencer's death in 1939, Charles Jr. continued to advise Julie in business matters.

Construction of the hotel began on May 20, 1917, and the company working on it claimed they could have it finished in a mere 350 days. When one considers how massive the Broadmoor is, this would have been quite a feat. However, the hotel would not officially open its doors to guests until June 29, 1918. There was a smaller, informal dinner held on June 1, but there were no overnight guests for the soft opening. Allegedly, some guests were supposed to stay in the hotel but could not handle the smell of the still-drying paint, and they were moved to the rival Antlers hotel. Once finished, the Broadmoor was called the most beautiful hotel in America by some, and the indoor swimming pool (which closed in 1961) was believed to be the largest pool in the United States at the time.

After Spencer's death, Charles Jr. took over much of the hotel's management, as the Penroses had no children together. Later,

Charles Jr.'s sons, Thayer and Russell, would take over respon-
sibilities for the hotel and surrounding amenities. It is said that
Thayer is largely responsible for continuing to build the hotel into
what it is today. Julie continued running the El Pomar charity
organization that she and Spencer founded and also funded the
building of a church and hospital in the city. She died in 1956 and
has a tomb in the Shrine of the Sun, along with Spencer.

Like its dedicated builder, the Broadmoor has legends surrounding it. At one point in the history of the property, the
lake had an out-of-control goldfish population, and the hotel
brought in sea lions to bring it back down. Unfortunately, sea
lions do not get as much nourishment from freshwater fish as
what they were accustomed to, and the upset animals caused
quite a ruckus on the hotel grounds. After several guest com-
plaints, hotel management decided to bring saltwater fish for
the sea lions every day.

Another favorite legend is Spencer's liquor collection. Before
Prohibition, he and many others in the country began buying
alcohol in large quantities so they would have a stash already
in place when the country went dry. Allegedly, Spencer's collection of booze was the largest in the United States. He was, in
any event, strongly against Prohibition and fought it until it was
repealed. Once it ended, he used his collection to throw quite the
party. Some of his collection nonetheless still remains and is on
display at the hotel, and some of it is even for sale in the hotel's
bar on the second floor for anyone will to pay quite the pretty
penny. In the hotel bar there are also paintings of Spencer along
the walls, one of them depicting him at the golf club. There are
several golf balls in the painting, but if you look closely, you will
notice that one of them is actually an eyeball, a bit of artistic
license that fits in with a story about Spencer and his glass eye.
Supposedly, he had several that varied in how bloodshot they
were, one for each level of drunk he could possibly be. As noted,

Spencer is a bit of a legend in Colorado Springs, and one who certainly knew how to have a good time.

Paranormal activity reported at the Broadmoor includes accounts of a female ghost walking about the hotel in clothing from the 1920s, and many think that it is the shade of Julie. It is also said that she most prominently haunts the suite where she and Spencer used to live. A legend concerning her death is that she had been missing for a week and then was found dead and naked in the forest behind the hotel. I could not find any verification of this, nor was it easy to find the true cause of Julie's death at all. Allegedly she died three weeks after having exploratory surgery. Instead of focusing on her death, however, most historical accounts prefer to shine light on all the charitable actions she made happen in the city of Colorado Springs.

Many believe there was a fire at the hotel that may be the cause of haunts in the building and say visitors can hear the screams of the victims of the fire. Longtime residents of the city, however, say there never was a fire at the Broadmoor and that it was the Antlers hotel that caught fire. Other paranormal episodes reported at the hotel involve unusual activity happening with lights in individual rooms and figures appearing in mirrors, and some say they were touched by unseen figures as well. Details aside, however, the owners of the Broadmoor are not very keen on the idea of it being haunted and generally shut down inquiries suggesting it might be. As it is one of the highest-rated hotels in Colorado, this is perhaps understandable from a business perspective.

A visit to the Broadmoor is nonetheless a must if you are in the Colorado Springs area, even if it just includes a walk around the lake. The hotel is a stunning location, particularly at Christmas, when the entire complex is decorated, complete with a life-size gingerbread house near the second-floor bar. Any paranormal investigation is best kept to individual rooms, however, as the hotel staff has been instructed to deny the ghostly rumors.

CHAPTER 16

Cave of the Winds
MANITOU SPRINGS

WHEN THINKING OF MOUNTAINS, one might also think of caves. Caves are an adventure to some, but for those who are not so fond of small spaces, they may be an experience to avoid. In fact, they have been the subject of numerous horror movies. Imagine crawling through narrow tunnels and hearing the echoes of sound that could be water dripping into a pool in the next cavern but that, in the dark, might be mistaken for voices. Shadows may move in unexpected ways in the small lights lining the walls of caves developed for visitors, and some may even have humanlike shapes. Determining which of the sounds and shadows are ghosts and which are your imagination can be nerve-wracking. In the Manitou Springs area, there is a potentially haunted system of caverns with an incredibly colorful history that is open to tourists, called the Cave of the Winds.

Cave of the Winds was discovered in what is now Williams Canyon in 1869 by a settler named Arthur B. Love. Its name comes from a legend told by the Jacarilla Apaches, who migrated through the area around what would become Pikes Peak, and revolves around the Great Spirit of the Wind they believed lived in a cave in the area. A paranormal research group called the Spirit-Chasers, founded in 2007 in Manitou Springs, claims that some of the caves that now make up the entire Cave of the Winds system were used by the Ute tribe as burial grounds, as the tribe believed the subterranean areas contained passageways to the underworld. In part the name also comes from the sound the wind makes as it passes the entrance. It is estimated that the limestone that forms the caves dates back nearly 500 million years, but the passages and rooms formed only 4–7 million years ago.

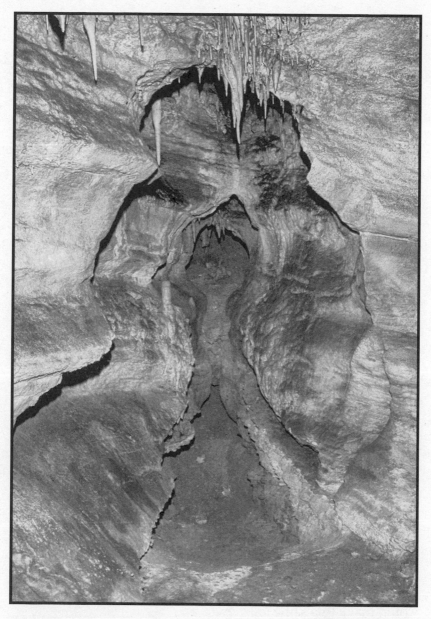

Cave of the Winds is estimated to have formed several million years ago.
During their first investigation of the caves, the Rocky Mountain Paranormal
Research Society had difficulties hooking up their electronics because the
wires were not long enough.

Even though the cave was discovered in 1869, it would not be until 1881 that it was permanently open for visitors. It had been open for a short time in 1880, but researchers from the Rocky Mountain Paranormal Research Society (RMPRS) believe that its high admission fee of $1 discouraged tourists. Before its opening, Cave of the Winds was featured in *Harper's Weekly* in October 1875 in the form of an engraving of a photograph by James Thurlow. Other caves in Williams Canyon began tours earlier than Cave of the Winds for admission fees somewhere around 50 cents, but they are no longer open to the public.

George Washington Snider discovered Canopy Hall, a section in the caves close to what is now the main tunnel entrance, while excavating the cave in the fall of 1880 with his acquaintance Charles Rinehart. It was Snider who started giving tours of the caves in February the next year at an admission cost of 50 cents. According to the RMPRS, Snider was unhappy with the business arrangement, as he paid most of the expenses and Rinehart received all the profit. So Snider began his own tours at a nearby cave he called Manitou Grand Caverns. The split eventually caused lawsuits between the two families, and these were appealed all the way to the Colorado Supreme Court, which decided not to hear the case. Final ruling was in favor of Rinehart, but he did not live to see it, and his children sought the profits of the suit.

While Cave of the Winds has been open to tourists since Snider's tours in early 1881, further exploration over the years has allowed expansion into different caverns and additional caves. In June 1895, a new entrance was created and later opened to the public. Its purpose was to allow customers to drive directly to the entrance of the cave in their carriages, and eventually cars would make this same journey.

During the winter months of 1905, efforts to restore the caves were undertaken and, in July 1907, electricity was brought into them for the first time. At the time, only Cave of the Winds

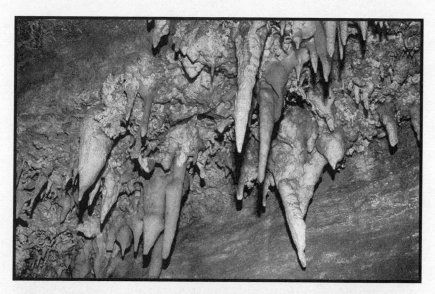

Stalactites, which hang from the ceiling, and other rock formations can be found in the Cave of the Winds. During tours, some guests claim to have seen or felt ghostly presences.

was running, as the company did not have enough money to light both Cave of the Winds and the Manitou Grand Caverns. This later led to the caverns being heavily vandalized, and eventually the company used dynamite to shut the entrance. Later, the owners widened the road for automobiles, and the tours continued to evolve throughout the 1900s as parts of the caves were discovered, closed, or created. New discoveries continued even into the mid-1980s. During World War II the location was considered for use as an air-raid shelter. It has also hosted several weddings throughout its commercial life. Cave of the Winds General Manager Daniel Carey also talked about a new activity, introduced in June 2015, in which guests are locked in one room and have to use clues to get themselves out.

Paranormal activity in the Cave of the Winds may be hard to determine. During its investigation of the site, RMPRS found that some of the tour guides admitted to making up some of their ghostly tales, presumably to please tourists who happen to have an interest in the paranormal. Some of the employees, however, genuinely believe the caves are haunted, and one of the more interesting reports involves extra people who have been seen following the tours when all guides and guests have been accounted for. Some of these reports describe the apparitions as being dressed in the attire that tour guides wear, and some say they are dressed in clothing from different time periods. Ghostly shapes have also been seen in the light of the lanterns, only to vanish upon further inspection.

Sounds are another frequently reported phenomenon, but for skeptics these may be the easiest to explain away. The story goes that several people have claimed to hear what sounded like an oncoming tour group, only to turn a corner and discover that there was nobody there. Voices and footsteps are also sometimes heard throughout the different caverns, which skeptics dismiss by saying that the acoustic quality of the caves causes sounds to travel. As a person who does not particularly like dark, small spaces, I imagine that my mind (and ears) would start to play some tricks on me if I let myself get carried away. During its investigation, however, the RMPRS had several investigators catch the sound of a violin playing in the concert hall. As there were no musicians there at the time, that particular episode is a little more difficult to dismiss. During their second investigation, RMPRS's Bryan Bonner and Matthew Baxter reported hearing what sounded like a motor running in the back of what is called Lover's Lane. Several of their investigators also reported seeing red lights on more than one occasion, and none of the group could find a reasonable explanation.

In late April 2012, the SpiritChasers were featured on The Biography Channel in a series called *My Ghost Story*. The group's particular episode, called "Whispering Walls," went into depth about reports of ghosts and other paranormal activity at

Cave of the Winds, as well as the cave's history with American Indian tribes (this episode can be found on YouTube). During their visits, group members have collected images with red orbs, smoky tendrils, and ghostly shapes that they believe to be Indian spirits. Paranormal activity reported to them includes people feeling breath on the back of their neck, clothing being tugged, whispers, shoulder taps, lanterns being blown out, and even the smell of roses.

Some people have reported seeing a strange woman sitting on rock shelves wearing a white dress. Some think the woman is Nellie, Snider's wife, as the pair often spent time in the caves looking for new passages. Snider himself is also thought to make appearances. Emergency call box employees claim to have received phone calls from an unidentified male, sometimes with just breathing on the other end, and some believe this to be the ghost of Snider. Rocks that have mysteriously been shifted around are also attributed to him, and some people think it is his way of continuing to care for the caves. The SpiritChasers believe that the ghostly figures in some of the images they have are actually Snider and his wife.

While a number of people believe the haunted activity at Cave of the Winds is authentic, skeptics might not find it easy to investigate. RMPRS had to do two investigations because the first time, it took far longer than they realized it would to set up all the wiring for computers, video cameras, and other electronic equipment. They were better prepared the second time and were able to do a longer investigation. Likewise, for paranormal enthusiasts who suffer from claustrophobia, this may be a hard location to explore for obvious reasons.

Regardless of whether you make it into the caves to investigate, you could not ask for a more beautiful setting to explore than Manitou Springs and the nearby city of Colorado Springs, both located in the heart of the mountains.

CHAPTER 17

Crawford Family
MANITOU SPRINGS

A rainstorm sent Emma Crawford's casket tumbling down the mountainside, and now residents of the city pay homage with an annual coffin race.

IN MANITOU SPRINGS, the name Crawford has become legend. Emma Crawford was a young woman who came to the city hoping that the dry mountain air and pure spring waters would help cure her tuberculosis. Later, her death and the unfortunate circumstance of multiple reinterments would spark coffin races and reenactments of her wake. Emma's ghost is said to be seen on her beloved Red Mountain, site of her original burial. Other members of the Crawford family allegedly haunt the area, as well, including Emma's sister, Alice Crawford Snow.

The Crawfords originally came from Massachusetts. Emma was born on March 24, 1863, and Alice was born on August 14, 1866. Their mother was a pianist known as Madame Jeanette Crawford, and both girls were musically oriented, with Emma considered a piano prodigy, playing pieces by Beethoven and Chopin at the age of 15. She frequently held piano concerts and also played the violin, viola, cello, and mandolin. Alice could also play, but her ambitions led her toward the stage. It was said that at a young age she ran away from her home in Massachusetts and police found her in New York looking for acting jobs.

At the age of 7, Emma was struck with what most people suspect to be tuberculosis, widely known at the time as consumption, and in 1889 the family relocated to Manitou Springs. They were not the only people flocking to the area in hopes that its namesake waters were as magically healing as others had led them to believe. In fact, it is estimated that nearly one-third of the residents at the time had come to the area to be cured of an illness.

The Crawfords settled in what was known as Castle Cottage, which was run as a boardinghouse. It had four rooms and was the first house to be built on what Manitou Springs residents call "Haunted Hill." Residents of the city believe that the town is a natural hot spot for ghosts, as it was cursed by American Indians. Madame Crawford was a spiritualist, as were her daughters; all three believed in ghosts, and the mother was known to host séances at the cottage.

Emma's particular fondness for ghosts came in the form of the "Red Chief," the name she gave nearby Red Mountain, as she believed the spirit of an Indian chief resided there. When she was not playing the piano, she could often be found enjoying nature. It became her dream to hike to the top of Red Mountain, but while Emma's health had improved dramatically, her family felt that she was still too frail to tackle such activity. Later, Emma fell in love with an engineer she had met in Boston named Wilhelm Hildebrandt. The young man followed her to Colorado, and eventually the pair became engaged and could frequently be seen walking together through town. Allegedly, Emma agreed to marriage only after her beloved promised to bury her at the top of Red Mountain if she should die before him. This request was borne from her fear of cemeteries, which represented strong sadness to Emma. She wanted instead to be buried somewhere where her spirit could be free, and to be one with nature and the mountain she loved so much.

Unfortunately for Emma, that day came before she was married. Her dreams of climbing the mountain had become overwhelming and, despite warnings from her doctor, family, and Hildebrandt, she attempted to summit its 7,375-foot peak. To make it, she would need to climb more than 900 feet from Manitou Springs' elevation of 6,412 feet. Emma did make it to the top of Red Mountain and, as the story goes, tied her handkerchief around a tree at the top and hurried down to tell everyone what she had accomplished. Later, a neighbor would venture to the top and find the handkerchief bearing Emma's initials, proving that the young woman really did climb to the top as she claimed. Upon her return, however, Emma was suffering from a fever and muttering that she had seen the Red Chief himself and that it was he who had led her to the top of the mountain; it may even have been his spirit that caused her sudden obsession with reaching the summit. As her last request, she asked Hildebrandt to honor his promise and said that she would wait for him at the top of the mountain.

Emma died on December 4, 1891. Hildebrandt and 11 others reportedly carried her casket to the top of Red Mountain, despite not being able to obtain a legal permit to bury her there, and worked in shifts to bury her in the cold, frozen mountainside. She stayed there until 1912, when her grave was moved to the

Emma Crawford's sister, Alice, is also said to haunt parts of Manitou. Alice stayed in the Red Stone Castle, now sometimes known as Crawford House, for a brief time while rehearsing for *Macbeth*. While the house is now a private residence, it is said that Alice haunts the Iron Mountains in the area.

south side of the mountain to make way for a railway incline. Then, in 1929, erosion finally caused her bones, nameplate, and silver casket handles—the only remaining pieces of her coffin—to slide down the mountainside.

Emma has allegedly haunted a couple of different places in Manitou Springs ever since. The most prevalent stories involve seeing her spirit on Red Mountain. Some claim to see her in a red dress, while others say she is wearing the wedding dress in which she was buried. And, while the cottage she lived in when she first moved to Manitou no longer has a piano in it, the sound of piano music has been heard in the house, and some claim to have seen Emma looking out the windows of the building.

After Emma died, her mother believed that she contacted her daughter many times via séances held in their home. During these events, Madame Crawford claimed that her daughter's

Colorado's Coffin Races

The Mile High State is home to not one but two unique races: the Emma Crawford Coffin Races in Manitou Springs and the Frozen Dead Guy Days in Nederland. These races are just what they sound like—teams running around carrying coffins from one place to another. But just how did these strange traditions start?

EMMA CRAWFORD COFFIN RACE

Manitou Springs is a small city located at the foot of Pikes Peak. People began flocking to the state in search of gold when Colorado first became a territory, and Pikes Peak in particular was the destination for many hopeful miners.

The sick came to Manitou Springs as well, as it was said that its mineral waters could help cure many ailments. Diagnosed with tuberculosis, Emma Crawford came with her family in the late 1800s. But her illness got the best of her in 1890 and she was buried on the slopes of Red Mountain. She did not stay in the location long, however; in 1912, she was moved to the south slope of the mountain. After a number of years, the harsh weather began to take its toll, and eventually Emma's grave resurfaced yet again, tumbling down the mountain during a storm. Her bones, nameplate, and silver casket handles were found by two local teenage boys. The idea of her grave contents sliding down the mountain is what inspired the races.

Since 1994, the coffin races have been held every year on the Saturday before Halloween. Each team consists of four runners and one "Emma," who sits in the constructed coffin. Runners push the coffin 195 feet, and the fastest team wins a trophy. Other prizes include best Emma, best entourage, and best coffin. The event starts with a parade of all the contestants, and there is also a showing of vintage hearses and a reenactment of Emma's wake, held at Miramont Castle. For more information, go to emmacrawfordfestival.com.

Frozen Dead Guy Days

Unlike the Emma Crawford event, which is only one day, Frozen Dead Guy Days in Nederland stretches over a weekend. In 2015, the 14th annual races were held in mid-March in honor of Bredo Morstoel, also known as "Grandpa Bredo." Morstoel's story is a science fiction mystery brought to life, as the man has been essentially an icicle since his death in 1989. After he died from a heart condition in Norway, his body was sent to California, where it was placed in liquid nitrogen. In 1993, he was sent to Colorado, where his daughter and grandson continued to keep him on ice.

One might well ask why someone would keep their dearly departed father on ice. Morstoel's living relatives were advocates of cryonics, a method of keeping bodies at very low temperatures in hopes of resuscitating them in the future. For years, Morstoel stayed in Colorado packed in ice. After his grandson was deported because his visa had expired, the dead man's daughter became his sole caretaker. She, however, was facing financial difficulties and was planning on returning to Norway. By contacting the local media, she was able to get the city to pass an ordinance addressing the keeping of bodies. It grandfathered Grandpa Bredo into it, and he has been in Nederland ever since. Some 1,600 pounds of dry ice are required to keep him at the necessary -60°F inside his sarcophagus, and the family has hired a man to change it monthly while they are in Norway.

In addition to the coffin race, the festival has live music, costume competitions (including a Grandpa Bredo lookalike contest), and more. Similar to the Emma Crawford race, a team member rides in the coffin, but at Frozen Dead Guy Days, six team members are required to carry the coffin, and they cannot drop it during the race. The top four teams race in a semifinal, and the two winners of that race compete for first place. At 8,400 feet above sea level, Nederland poses a challenge. Throw in a little snow for good measure, and the spirit of the Frozen Dead Guy Days festival is quite tangible. For more information, go to frozendeadguydays.org.

spirit came alive through her and would begin to play the piano. Alice and her mother did not remain long in the city after Emma's death but did return on several occasions. They moved first to Los Angeles, where Alice attempted to start her acting career, and then later returned to Massachusetts, where Alice picked up some Shakespearean work and possibly a few husbands. There is record of her marrying Theodore Snow, a businessman, but some historians suspect she was married to someone else before that as well. In 1898 she had a daughter named Maurine by one of these men.

In 1910, Alice returned to Manitou Springs alone. She rented the Red Stone Castle (not to be confused with the Manitou Springs hotel the Redstone Castle) to prepare for an audition in Denver. The house would later be known as the Crawford House and may be where Alice's spirit made its permanent home. The role Alice was so desperately auditioning for was that of Lady Macbeth. Known to be a method actress, she could be seen dressing in long, white robes to prepare. Food and firewood were delivered to the house on Mondays, but outside of that the gates were locked, and she frequently wandered the Iron and Red Mountains in solitude. As a result of Alice's crazed activity, friends in the area stopped coming to see her. Additionally, the store sending deliveries had difficulty getting people to take on the task, as Alice allegedly insisted they address her as Lady Macbeth and spoke to them only in iambic pentameter. In particular, delivery boys claimed to hear her screaming, "Out, damned spot!" a famous line from the play *Macbeth*.

Alice, like Emma, believed in ghosts and felt that Red Stone Castle was haunted. In a strange incident in which her friend found her with a gunshot kneecap and her bed on fire, Alice tried to claim that it had all been caused by ghosts. Many people, however, believed that Alice had become mentally unstable and may have tried to commit suicide, and is it rumored that after not receiving the role of Lady Macbeth she wrote to a friend saying it was all over. In February 1910, the *Colorado Springs Gazette Telegraph* reported that Madame Crawford had returned to care for her daughter and that she believed Alice had also been worrying about the state of her finances. After being released from the hospital, Alice never returned to Manitou Springs.

While the Red Stone Castle is now a private residence, it used to operate as a bed-and-breakfast. Before Alice rented the home alone, the Crawfords had previously rented it on several of their trips to Manitou. Their numerous séances, performed in attempts to speak with the departed Emma, were what helped give the house its haunted reputation. It was in this house that Madame Crawford claimed Emma's spirit possessed her in order to play the piano, and where guests have claimed to hear piano music and what sounded like a woman speaking lines from *Macbeth*.

Some people claim that not only does Alice haunt the castle but she may haunt Iron Mountain as well. There are no claims that Madame Crawford has joined her daughters in haunting the mountain town where all three resided, but she did outlive both of them and continued playing piano on the East Coast for some time.

CHAPTER 18

Miramont Castle
MANITOU SPRINGS

This former home of a Catholic priest, on the National Register of Historic Places, is now a museum.

"KEEP MANITOU WEIRD" is a slogan that explains a lot about this small mountain town, such as its annual reenactment of the wake of Emma Crawford every year at Miramont Castle, the local historical museum. Crawford, who has been dead for more than 100 years, is also the subject of the annual Emma Crawford Coffin Race. While it is rumored that she haunts parts of the city and its neighboring Red Mountain, she is not the only specter to make an appearance in Manitou Springs. Indeed, Miramont Castle functions as more than a piece of the spectacle that is the Emma Crawford Festival; it was once a hospital for tuberculosis patients that was run by a group of nuns. The ghost of one of these nuns, called Henrietta by employees, may still wander the halls of the old castle.

Before the castle was built, the land it stands on was owned by Col. John M. Chivington, a dark and controversial character in Colorado's history. Originally known for saving Colorado from invasion during the Civil War, he would later become more infamously known as the lead military figure in the Sand Creek Massacre (page 94). His deed to the land is originally dated 1862, and his son-in-law sold it with power of attorney in 1867, although Chivington would later sue, saying he did not grant this. Chivington did not win the case, and the land moved through the hands of various owners until it was eventually sold to the city of Manitou Springs in 1882.

By some means lost to history, a priest named Father Jean Baptiste Francolon acquired the lands and began to design a castle inspired by his travels around the world with his father, who had been a diplomat. Francolon came to the United States from Europe in 1878 and, after spending some time working in New Mexico, came to Manitou Springs for his health, often complaining of abdominal pains. The castle appears to be his only legacy, as according to some sources he was a loner and not popular with the locals (although a varying account says he frequently played piano at parties).

Construction on the main section of the castle began in 1895, and on the eastern section of the building two years later. When completed, Miramont, which means "look at the mountain," had both indoor plumbing and electricity. Francolon's widowed mother, Marie, came to live in the castle with him and had a suite on the third floor.

Once it was completed, the castle featured nine architectural styles. With four floors, more than 40 rooms, and 14,000 square feet, the building nonetheless has few rooms with four square corners. Among its unusually shaped spaces are an 8-sided room and 16-sided room. Because the building sits on a mountainside, the front entrance sits on the first floor, but the rear entrance is on the fourth floor. This created a stair-like structure, and each floor had an exit onto the ground level outside. The building was probably finished sometime near the end of 1896. The first official event held there was a charity costume ball in January 1897.

Francolon would not stay in the completed castle long; he left for France unexpectedly in 1900 and never returned to Colorado. There are many theories as to why Francolon departed, the main one being that the Mother Superior of the area, a Mother Baptist, accused Francolon of accosting children and threatened to expose him. Supposedly he cursed her, telling her she would die within a year, and then fled. Coincidentally or not, Mother Baptist did die in a train wreck in August 1901.

The Sisters of Mercy also came to Manitou in 1895 at the request of Francolon. He donated his old home, which was on the same land as the Miramont, as a space for them to create a sanitarium for the large influx of tuberculosis patients who made their way to the city for its "healing waters." The hospital was called the Montcalme Sanitarium, and while Francolon was still in Manitou he acted as president of the organization. The sisters took their first patient in August, and by March of the next year needed to expand the building to meet demand. The only time the sisters would not help a patient was if the case was acute; in that event, they recommended the patient go to nearby Colorado Springs.

The castle remained vacant for four years after Francolon's departure in 1900, until the sisters purchased it in 1904 in hopes of using it for water therapy treatments, but this idea never came to fruition. In 1907, an electrical fire destroyed the old hospital building, and the sisters formally moved into Miramont Castle, where they served the community for 20 years. They kept the name Montcalme Sanitarium but needed to make several changes to the castle to convert it into a functioning hospital. The original building for the sanitarium stood where the upper parking lot of the museum is now, and in its far corner stands one of the old isolation huts for tuberculosis patients, the only part of the sanitarium still standing. While Francolon was living in the building with his mother, there was an elaborate tunnel system beneath the castle that connected it to the sanitarium, which the sisters used to deliver meals. There were also rumored to be secret staircases and corridors throughout the building.

While things ran smoothly for the most part for the sisters, there was one who had a secret. Her name was Henrietta, and she had become pregnant by a priest. She allegedly went to the priest in question to get his help with the baby and asked him to leave the priesthood and marry her, but he refused. Some suspect that the priest may have been Francolon. From here, the story goes that Henrietta tied a noose around her neck, tied the other end of the rope to a radiator, and leaped from one of the windows. Supposedly she leaped from the third-floor solarium, and according to the legend, the force of the rope was so strong that she was decapitated. Several employees at the Miramont have reported seeing her headless ghost wandering the building.

Unfortunately for the sisters, in 1928 they were no longer financially able to keep running the hospital and had to shut it down. They split the building into 10 apartments and remained in it until 1946, renting the rooms to wealthy tourists or to visiting religious figures. After that, Miramont Castle passed on to private owners, who kept the apartment style of the building and continued leasing it. In 1971, the Manitou Springs Historical Society was formed and unanimously decided that they would make the building their home to preserve the city's Victorian heritage and role as a hub of cultural history.

By 1976, there was a fear that the building could be demolished. To save it from being destroyed, 26 families in Manitou Springs took out mortgages on their homes. They were led by Lillian and Ivan Graggs, to whom a section of the museum is now dedicated. They purchased the building on February 17, 1976. Through the help of Philip Lawrence Hannum, they were able to qualify for the $7,500 Centennial-Bicentennial Grant to restore the castle. Hannum went through the building, taking hundreds of photographs, which he used to create detailed instructions on how to renovate individual areas of the hotel. The photographs were compared to other pictures of the hotel from when it was first built to ensure the building would be restored as close to its original state as possible. The town raised an additional amount to help in the process as well, and many of the people who came to restore the castle were volunteers. In fact, the city estimates that 95% of the workers were from volunteer groups. Their hard work was rewarded, and the building was given national landmark status on May 3, 1977.

While the rest of the ghost stories are not nearly as gruesome as Henrietta's, there are others. One spirit encountered frequently is the ghost of a young girl who is seen in the gift shop and, as with many of the sightings in the building, seems to be from the Victorian era. She is frequently seen carrying a doll, and some think she may be the spirit of one of the sisters' patients. A Victorian-era couple has also been seen in the building. A widowed woman in a black dress and veil will sometimes appear specifically in the mirrors; lights throughout the building will reportedly turn off and on by themselves; sometimes the mannequins will change positions overnight; some claim to hear singing in the chapel area when no one is around; and piano music can also be heard. Because of all this, some of the volunteers and staff members will allegedly not enter certain rooms.

It is no mystery to most of the people of Manitou Springs as to why their small town has such a large number of ghosts. Manitou means Great Spirit, and the land it is on was first inhabited by American Indian tribes who believed the land to be sacred. People residing there today feel the same way, and many of them continue to enjoy the spiritual energy of the city.

CHAPTER 19

Museum of Colorado Prisons
CAÑON CITY

Home to seven prisons, Cañon City, Colorado, also features the Museum of Colorado Prisons, which was once a women's prison.

A MUSEUM DEDICATED STRICTLY TO prison life may seem like a strange idea, but bear with Colorado on this one. Since opening in 1988, the Museum of Colorado Prisons has reported serving more than 200,000 people. Their clever slogan, "Come do time with us," gives a little insight on what visitors can do in this museum. Exhibits feature 30 old cells on the upper floor, each of which has a story about past inmates. Inmates featured include Alferd Packer, one of the first men to be tried for cannibalism in the United States, and Anton Woode, a 12-year-old boy convicted of murder. He was the youngest person ever incarcerated in the United States at the time. Other exhibits, such as the last gas chamber built in Colorado, are meant to remind the visitors that crime always comes with punishment. It is no surprise that the museum of prison life found its home in Cañon City, which is also known as Prison City. The city houses seven of Colorado's 20 public prisons, one of which, the Colorado Territorial Correctional Facility, has been open since 1871. It opened while Colorado was still a territory. Originally it was called the Colorado State Penitentiary and would house Packer while he served his time for murder. The name changed to CTCF in January 1979. At one point the city had the highest per capita prison rate, not just in the nation but in the world.

Colorado, like all states, is not without its bizarre and unfortunate history. One of the strange facts you will come across when researching Colorado is it was home to one of the larger cannibalism cases in the United States. While cases of cannibalism remain few, Packer's story has become the stuff of legend in the state. Mad Greens, a local sandwich and salad café, has even named a seasonal menu item after him.

Born in Pennsylvania in January 1842, Packer was the son of a cabinetmaker. He enlisted in the army during the Civil War in 1862 and was honorably discharged due to struggles with epilepsy. After leaving the army, Packer worked mining jobs for nine years. While working as a miner in Sandy, Utah, he learned of the gold strikes happening in the San Juan Mountains of Colorado. He decided to join a small group of men who began organizing a trip to Colorado. Packer, who was quite poor at the time, did not have the $50 that paid for transportation and provisions. Instead, it was agreed that he would pay $25 and work for the rest by tending to the team's horses on the journey. They left Provo, Utah, in 1873 with 21 men.

Not long into their journey, they began to run low on food and survived off the barley they had brought for the horses, as game was also scarce. Once they reached Colorado they were brought to Chief Ouray, a leader of the Ute tribe. Ouray was well known for his negotiations with the Americans for tribal lands. The chief let the weary travelers rest with his people for some time. He gave them directions to Los Pinos Agency, where they could stop and get provisions; however, he warned them to wait. Ouray knew that mountain travel could be treacherous at this time of year due to snowy weather. His directions allotted a week of travel to get to Los Pinos. After several debates and arguments among the group, five of them left on February 6. They reached Los Pinos three weeks later.

On February 9, Packer left the camp with his group of six. Almost immediately they hit the bad weather Ouray had warned them about and were caught in a snowstorm. Packer would not arrive in Los Pinos until April 16. He was the only one who made it.

Because the first group had already arrived, the small town was expecting more people and questioned Packer on the location of the rest of his party. Packer claimed that an injured leg prevented him from going with the whole group and that he let them go ahead of him. He spent quite a bit of time in both Los Pinos and Saguache repeating his story to anyone who would listen, but the rest of the party never arrived. Other members of the original group also began to notice that Packer was no longer poor and was now carrying a knife that he hadn't had before, one that belonged to another person in Packer's party. Suspecting Packer of foul play, the men of the town suggested that Packer lead a group back down the same route he had taken to Los Pinos in the hopes of finding the rest of his men.

During the search for the group, Packer became confused and claimed he could not remember the route. Upon their return the search party arrested him on suspicion of homicide even though they had not recovered the bodies. Once arrested, Packer changed his story. He said that one by one the men in his group began dying from the cold. The first to die was eaten by the party, as were the second and third. Of the remaining three survivors, one killed the other and then went after Packer, who shot the man in self-defense. In August 1874 the bodies were found.

All were missing their personal effects, such as money and other provisions. They were also well preserved in the snow and it was clear the victims had been mutilated and suffered blows. The area where the bodies were found was renamed Dead Man's Gulch. A new warrant was issued for five counts of murder, but by then Packer had escaped from his cell.

He would not be arrested again until March 1883, when he was found by chance in Fort Fetterman. His second confession said he had gone in search of food for the group, only to return to find four of the party members killed and the fifth cooking them over a fire. The man began to attack Packer, but Packer shot him. He continued by saying he survived the next 60 days by eating his companions. His trial began that April, and people began to call for a death by hanging. Although he was convicted of the murder of one party member and sentenced to hang, he was granted a retrial. There is debate on the spelling of his name, but his execution invitations (before the retrial) were printed with the name "Alferd." His appeal was brought before the Colorado Supreme Court in Gunnison in 1886. He was found guilty of manslaughter and received a sentence of 40 years in the state penitentiary in Cañon City, 13 years after the crime. After only 15 years of this sentence, he was granted parole by Gov. Charles S. Thomas due to his age and physical condition. He later died after an epileptic attack in 1907.

Packer is one of the famed inmates featured in an exhibit at the Museum of Colorado Prisons. The building the museum now resides in was once the women's prison, which was constructed in 1935. The citizens of Fremont County came up with the concept of the museum in the 1980s. In April 1986 the Colorado legislature approved the idea and funded Cañon City's plans to create the museum. The women's prison was leased to the foundation, creating the museum for 99 years. The building is next to the CTCF, which still operates as a prison. The facility is sometimes called "Old Max" as it is the oldest prison in Colorado. It is capable of holding 930 prisoners. The museum was ready to open in June 1988 once renovations and adjustments were made, making the old women's prison more accessible to visitors.

Some of the items exhibited include the noose from the last executional hanging in Colorado, as well as weapons and other items confiscated from prisoners over the 141 years of prison history in the state. The museum includes an audio tour with descriptions of these items. The museum also holds paranormal investigation nights, though their list of available dates on the website has not been updated since 2013. I recommend their Facebook page for a more recent schedule of these tours. The investigations are of the museum building, but some include a visit to the nearby Woodpecker Hill Cemetery. Many of the inmates were buried here, but you won't find them by name. Their grave markers feature only their prison number.

Of the haunted incidents in the museum, most accounts center around cell 19 and the kitchen area. The sound of a woman coughing can sometimes be heard in cell 19. It is thought that it could be the spirit of an inmate who died there. There was also a woman involved in some sort of knife fight in the kitchen area. Some people have felt light pushes in the room. On the ground level, there is an outdoor courtyard area where people can walk into the tiny cells. The cells were used when the building was a prison and cannot be much larger than 8 square feet. Next to the courtyard is the large wall built to keep in the inmates of CTCF. It is topped with strings of barbed wire. In these conditions it is easy for visitors to get a feel for what prison life really is. One can also be a little more understanding of why the miserable souls may have never left.

West

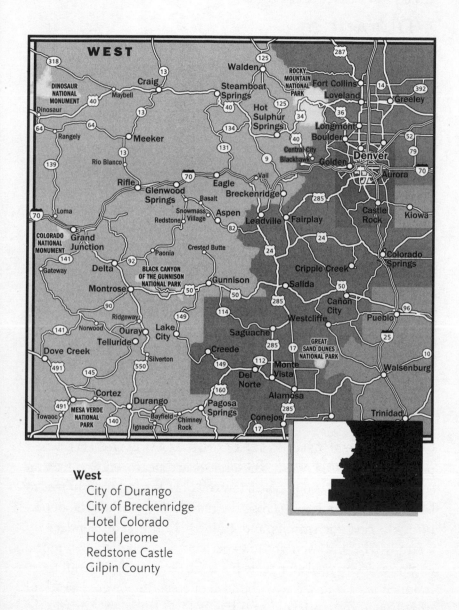

West
- City of Durango
- City of Breckenridge
- Hotel Colorado
- Hotel Jerome
- Redstone Castle
- Gilpin County

CHAPTER 20

City of Durango

DURANGO

A Durango & Silverton Narrow Gauge Railroad train makes a flag stop near Needleton, Colorado.

ONE OF THE THINGS PEOPLE MAY IMAGINE when picturing the Wild West is a large black steam engine tearing across the plains, and maybe a few cowboys forcing their horses to keep up. Many railways across the nation give tourists the opportunity to ride such trains and I did this once as a teenager on a family trip, and even got to experience a cowboy following the engine as it chugged alongside his land. Once aboard one of these trains, it is easy to see why the idea of a steam-powered hunk of iron was so romanticized and has held to this day. Apparently, some spirits may feel the same way, finding it hard to let go of the iron horse and its glory days.

If you should become tired of hearing about towns being founded by pioneers searching for gold and silver, then make Durango your next stop. Durango was founded by the Denver and Rio Grande Railroad (D&RG) after a different Colorado town, Animas City, refused to pay a dowry to have the company's depot located in their city. Durango was founded in September 1881 and named after Durango, Mexico, which was itself named after Durango, Spain. The word durango roughly means "water town," a strange title in that a large portion of Colorado falls into what was considered the Great American Desert. The Animas River, however, flows through the city's downtown area, which may be where the name came from. Although the town was not founded by miners, it did receive quite the economic boost from their presence and rivaled Leadville as one of the top mining cities in Colorado.

Before the city of Durango was officially founded, the railroad was formally brought into the area in August 1881. That fall the city began a narrow-gauge line to the city of Silverton, Colorado, which is almost directly north of Durango. Narrow-gauge railroads are so called because their tracks are more narrow than those of standard railways, and their materials are a little bit lighter, which made it slightly cheaper for companies to build this kind of track. Construction of the Silverton line was completed in July 1882 and it was used to move both freight and passenger cars. While the track was primarily built to transport silver and gold ore—estimates are that more than 300 million dollar's worth of those precious metals were transported over this route—it was also advertised as a scenic line for tourists traveling through the San Juan Mountains and was promoted with the motto "through the Rockies, not around them." Creating tracks through the granite-filled mountains was surely not an easy task, but the

A train for the Durango & Silverton Narrow Gauge Railroad sits at the railroad station in Silverton. Baldwin Locomotive Works built this K-36 class steam locomotive for the Denver & Rio Grande Western Railroad in 1925.

scenic views that brought tourists to the city was thought to be worth it. Other railroad companies began expanding and a track to the city of Ouray, Colorado, was added in 1887.

But the glory years of the mines and railroads would soon come to an end with the silver crash in 1893 that devastated much of the state's economy. This was just the first hardship that the railroad line had to face. In 1901, the D&GR merged with the Rio Grande Western and the two companies were consolidated in 1908. There was a tourist bump in 1906 when Mesa Verde became a national park, but it was not enough. The railway faced financial hardships as well, as floods and rock slides, which had the potential to inflict lots of damage to the tracks. Shortly after the merger of the two companies their finances continued to weaken. Then, during World War I, the government seized control of all the railroads in the United States. After the war, when the railroads were back in the control of their respective companies, D&GR went into receivership and was reorganized in

1921 as the Denver & Rio Grande Western Railroad (D&RGW). Spanish Flu hit Silverton in 1918, killing 10 percent of the city's population in a matter of weeks. This, along with closures of a couple mines in the area, caused the Silverton railroad to close.

Durango was reinvigorated during World War II, when the smelter reopened and began to process uranium. This continued past the end of the war and continued into the Cold War. Hollywood helped to bring tourists back to Durango after filming several westerns there, and the line was made a national historic landmark in the '60s. Eventually, the tracks were repaired, along with train cars that had not been used in as many as 20 years, which were upgraded and renovated so that they could be used in the winter. The goal was to make the trains usable again as a tourist attraction and they were being refurbished for use on a scenic train route.

Today, American Heritage Railways operates four trains year-round on the original line, which is now are more than 120 years old. In traditional fashion, the locomotives that pull the cars are steam-powered with coal, and there is a museum dedicated to the tracks next to the train depot in Durango. Once aboard the train, it is a three-and-half-hour ride to Silverton. One of the scenic views on the ride is known as "The Million Dollar Highway" for its spectacular views of the Rocky Mountains. American Heritage Railways has also partnered with True West Magazine and played host to the True West Railfest, which includes Wild West shows, teaches visitors about railroad equipment, and has a murder-mystery train ride.

In October 2014, the train had a ride called Tales of Morticians that coincided with the release of the book *Ghost Tracks: Haunting Tales Along the Rails* by Elizabeth A. Green and Suzy Garrison Meyer. The book gives more information on ghost tales associated with the line and the tour guide portrays a family member of the Goodmans, Durango's family of morticians. During the holiday season, the train has also been used for a ride based on the popular children's book *The Polar Express,* and the story is read aloud to passengers in pajamas while they drink hot cocoa.

Strange and unexplainable occurrences have been known to happen on the railway line, both at the depot and even along the ride, and people claim to have both seen and heard spirits in areas around the tracks. One of the more popular ghosts people talk about is the apparition of a man in overalls. Supposedly those who see him claim that he floats along the tracks and the railroad's old roundhouse in Durango, which was originally built in 1882 and had 10 stalls to house the locomotives that were not in use. There was a fire that nearly destroyed all of Durango in 1889 which, along with most of the city, also claimed the roundhouse. It was rebuilt with 18 stalls and this is the structure that still stands today, although some of the stalls have been demolished or converted to storage. This particular ghost's reason for floating is not because that is what all the cool Hollywood ghosts do, but rather because he lost his legs in a train accident. Children have also been heard running around the area and causing havoc such as breaking windows around stationary train cars, but employees that go to chase off these miscreants can never seem to find them. Floating lanterns have been seen along the tracks, carried by unseen people. Many train riders also claim to have been touched by unseen hands while riding on the train.

The Rocky Mountains are a beautiful, and sometimes intimidating place and the days of the Iron Horse were not easy for most Coloradans. In many ways, building a railroad through miles of rock could have been a task that took a builder's life, and one might well wonder how many of them decided to linger and see the finished product. Although there are many ways to travel through and see colorful Colorado, taking the train through its mountains is certainly a unique way to do

A mother-and-son team renovated the Rochester Hotel and decorated its various rooms with Wild West themes.

it. After all, how many states can claim a scenic route with a million-dollar view, and has ghosts to boot?

ROCHESTER HOTEL

SHORTLY AFTER THE FOUNDING of Durango in 1881, the Rochester Hotel came to be. It is now family-owned and -operated by a mother–son duo, Diane Wildfang and Kirk Komick, who renovated both the Rochester and a separate property, the Leland House. The Rochester has been re-done in the style of classic Wild West movies, giving it the nickname "Hollywood of the West." This theme was selected because several movie companies took advantage of the high rising mountains, local ranches, and even the railroad itself for filming Western-themed movies. Each room has a theme based on Hollywood's Wild West, and some, such as room 204, which is known as the "John Wayne Room," honor specific actors. It is in this room that the majority of the hotel's haunted reports come from.

In Linda R. Wommack's book Colorado's Landmark Hotels, she calls the Rochester "an accidental tourist attraction." Durango is not an area that many tourists would think to seek out, except maybe for skiing in the winter, and the 2010 census reported the city to have 16,887 people, so this is the destination you should look at if you do not like big crowds.

Like many areas of Colorado, there is a great risk of forest fires in the summer, and it was a blaze of this sort that nearly destroyed the city in July of 1889. It was atop the ashes of this fire that the foundations of the Rochester were erected. The land was purchased from one of the founders of the D&RG and construction began in 1890 on what was originally going to be called the Peeples Hotel. Despite problems with financial backing and ownership changes, the hotel opened its doors in 1892. Its success, however, was short lived and, like an unfortunate number of hotels and cities throughout the state, it suffered greatly during the silver crash in 1893.

Although the hotel survived the crash, it did not thrive. Tourism in Durango depended largely on the railroad and, when daily connections began again in 1895, new guests began to frequent the hotel. In 1905, the property changed hands once again and was renamed the Rochester Hotel. Its owner at the time began several renovations that added more space in the hotel's 33 rooms by extending the front of the building to the sidewalk.

Wildfang and Komick purchased the building in 1992. Their renovations were considerably more extensive and lasted for two years. While they kept much of the original furniture and woodwork, such as doors and trim, the new owners reduced the number of rooms to 15 and designed them to be more spacious and for each to include a private bathroom.

During the renovations there were several odd reports from contractors, many of whom quit their jobs, claiming they did not feel comfortable in the building. The most common report of ghosts in the hotel is of a Victorian woman who is seen in room 204, the "John Wayne Room." She is either seen in a dress or, as some more scandalous reports claim, lingerie. Other reports include doors locking on their own and items moving of their own accord. In a 2009 article for *The Durango Telegraph,* Fred Wildfang, Diane's husband, claimed that the Rochester is on a top 100 list most-haunted hotels (although he did not specify who published this list and I could not find it).

Durango is fairly far off the beaten path. However, if you are specifically looking for a small mountain town, you can put your money on this one. While there are several mountain towns sprinkled around the state, there are not many that offer a haunted hotel and train as well, along with what some say is the most intense skiing in the nation.

CHAPTER 21

City of Breckenridge

BRECKENRIDGE

The Historic Brown Hotel & Restaurant, built in the 1880s, featured the first bathtub in Summit County. Constructed as a private dwelling, it was once operated as a school by Union Captain George L. Ryan and his wife and later as a hotel by Maude and Tom Brown.

BRECKENRIDGE IS ONE OF THE MANY ski resort towns in the Rocky Mountain State. Like many Colorado cities, it was founded by prospectors who came to the mountains seeking a fortune during the gold rush. It was founded in 1859 and named for John C. Breckinridge, who at the time was serving as vice president of the United States. Town founders hoped that the name of the city would flatter the government so they could gain a post office and become a city faster, and the idea worked. Once the Civil War broke out, however, Breckinridge announced that he was siding with the Confederacy, prompting the pro-Union citizens of the town to change the first *i* in its name to an *e*.

Shortly after the establishment of the settlement, a new map of the United States was printed, and Breckenridge was accidentally left off of it, a mistake that was not noticed for nearly 50 years. During this time the city became known as "Colorado's Kingdom" and still celebrates this with the Kingdom Days festival dedicated to the heritage of Breckenridge. Breckenridge is, in fact, very proud of its origins and history and claims to have one of the largest historic districts in Colorado, with more than 200 locations listed on the National Register of Historic Places. There are also frequent historic tours of the city.

One of the little-known facts about ski towns in Colorado is that during the summer months many of them become like ghost towns, and some restaurants and shops even close for the season. Hotels still have some business from people searching for summertime weekend mountain escapes and ambitious travelers looking to climb fourteeners (mountains with an elevation of 14,000 feet or more). Although "Breck," as it is called locally, seems to be less booming in the summer, it is not quite a ghost town and is one of the communities that can boast water activity in the summer months, with whitewater rafting being only one of the options. It also has its Fun Park, spas, and golfing.

Although it may not be a literal ghost town in the summer, the city does claim to have some ghostly residents and even offers ghost tours through the "haunted historic district" of Breckenridge. Many of them include a stop at The Historic Brown Hotel & Restaurant, which is supposedly haunted by a ghost known throughout the city as "the lady of the night."

THE HISTORIC BROWN HOTEL
& RESTAURANT

NOT TO BE CONFUSED WITH the Brown Palace Hotel
in Denver (although both may be haunted), The Historic Brown
Hotel & Restaurant is located in the more mountainous city of
Breckenridge. The original date it was built is a mystery, even
to historians. They believe it was constructed sometime in the
1800s as a private residence and then later used as a school
until 1882, when it opened its doors as a hotel. As with all hotels
that have a haunted reputation in Colorado, I have begun to ask
myself just how haunted these places really are and how much
of it is the owner seeking to capitalize on the world's current
fascination with the paranormal.

Many of the historic tours offered in Breckenridge that
include the Brown hotel as a stop are actually run by the
Breckenridge Heritage Alliance (breckheritage.com). In fact,
hotel owner Michael Cavanaugh was interviewed by the
Summit Daily News for an article that came out in October 2010,
and it seems that he has no interest in the alleged paranormal
activity at his business. He even offered a few logical explanations for it. However, the popularity of the "lady of the night"
has prevailed, and the tours continue to come through, even five
years after publication of the article.

Exactly who was the "lady of the night" that haunts the
hotel? She was known simply as Ms. Whitney and was exactly
what her nickname suggests: a prostitute. Supposedly, she lived
in Breckenridge sometime between the late 1800s and the early
1900s and wanted to use the Brown Hotel to further her business and expand her clientele. To sweet-talk the owner into letting her use the building for her business, she began sleeping
with him. Once the man caught wind of her plans, however, and
that she was sleeping around with other men, he allegedly shot

her. These events had to occur after 1882, if they happened at all, as the location was not even a hotel until that point.

Ms. Whitney is said to still reside in the building in a more ghostly form. So strong are the stories of her haunting the women's restroom that some women have refused to enter the room alone. Faucets have been known to turn on and off on their own, and the curtains have also been known to move.

This "lady of the night" seems to be the only entity that appears in the Historic Brown, and all other accounts of paranormal activity are about objects moving on their own, lights flickering, doors slamming, and the like. Ms. Whitney, however, does not seem to lack company in the mountain town, and with a constant stream of tours coming to the hotel in addition to the guests, there are always plenty of people to see.

COUNTRY BOY MINE

ONCE THE SILVER INDUSTRY went bust in Colorado, many of the mines that caused the state to thrive for so long began to shut down. Some lucky mines came to life again during the World Wars, but very few of them are still in use today. Some mines, however, such as the Country Boy Mine in Breckenridge, are now open for tourists to visit.

Founded in 1887, Country Boy Mine was famous for its gold and silver production and is one of the oldest mines in Summit County. In 1860, gold was discovered in the area, known as the French Gulch, which was home to several other important mines during that era. The largest piece of gold in the state was mined from the French Gulch. It was not a nugget (a deposit formed by several years of being worn down by water) but rather a 13.5-pound piece of the much rarer crystallized lode gold. The prospector who discovered it was known to carry it around wrapped in a blanket like a baby, and thus the find is known today as Tom's Baby.

At one point, nearly 8,000 prospectors had made their way to Breckenridge and other parts of Summit County in the hopes of finding gold. Later, in World Wars I and II, the Country Boy Mine was a large producer of high-grade lead and zinc. It shut down for a time between the wars and closed permanently in 1948.

In 1991, Doug and David Tomlinson decided to restore the Country Boy Mine to its historical glory. Their intent was to preserve the mining history of Colorado and the impact that mines had in pioneering the West; it reopened to the public in 1994. In addition to touring the mine, visitors can pan for gold and visit other areas in the mine site, which still features some of the old buildings and equipment from the original mine. The exhibits feature photographs and historical information as well.

Mining was not all gold and riches, especially back in the days of the gold rush. Miners faced difficulties on a daily basis, and it was not unusual for them to die on the job. Explosions, difficulties with equipment, and cave-ins were just some of the things that could take a miner's life. Some people believe the spirits of some of those workers might still linger at the Country Boy Mine. Guests of the tours have begun to realize that strange objects show up in the photographs they take at the mines, including orbs and distinctly human-shaped apparitions. In some of these photographs, one can even see the shape of a beard. A previous owner, Paul Hintgen, has also said that his tour guides would report being shoved while checking the air levels in the mines by themselves. Could it be that the draw of gold is so great that the ghosts of killed miners chose to stay forever?

SYLVIA THE GHOST

UNTIL RECENTLY, there was an establishment called the Prospector Restaurant located on 130 S. Main St. in Breckenridge. From what I can tell, the business under that name closed sometime after May 2015, as an article from the *Summit Daily News* published on May 8 of that year still identifies the location as the Prospector Restaurant. My guess is that it closed for the season and was unable to reopen. There is, however, a new restaurant at the same address called Après Handcrafted Libations. There is said to be a ghost by the name of Sylvia residing in the building. Local legend has it that she is searching for a husband.

In 1892, Harry and Jennie Whitehead built the Arcade Hotel. Unfortunately, the business soon failed. Jennie tried again in 1902 and opened the building as a boardinghouse and restaurant, and since then it has been used as an eatery in Breckenridge.

The legend of Sylvia was also born here and, like the Brown Hotel, the restaurant is a stop on Breckenridge's haunted tours. Sylvia, unlike Ms. Whitney at the Brown, does not have a violent past. She was the widow of a miner in the area and supposedly lived in the boardinghouse there. For a long time, the ghost was reported to be seen only by men, purportedly because Sylvia was searching for a new, rich husband. Some believe her ghost is still on the prowl, a new version of a cougar, so to speak. Bad jokes aside, according to the *Summit Daily News,* she was sometimes reported to have folded the clothes of ski bums living in the boardinghouse. However, according to the same article, she has evolved and started showing herself to more people, including women. Some say they simply feel a presence, some have heard what sounds like ruffling skirts, and others have reported books coming off the shelves by themselves.

Breckenridge is surely a place to visit in Colorado, especially if you want to visit the mountains and ski in the winter. While in the city, paranormal enthusiasts can either opt for the guided tour or create their own by visiting the haunted sites there. The day can begin with a tour of the Country Boy Mine, move on to dinner at The Historic Brown Hotel & Restaurant, and then end with ghostly cocktails at Après Handcrafted Libations. After all, you will hear skiing locals use the term *après vous* to mean drinks after a day of skiing, although the literal French translation is "after you."

CHAPTER 22

Hotel Colorado

GLENWOOD SPRINGS

Hotel Colorado in Glenwood Springs has been open for more than 100 years and was frequently used by Theodore Roosevelt during his stays in Colorado. Several apparitions are thought to haunt the hotel.

THE HOTEL COLORADO OPENED just before the turn of the century in 1893 and has hosted many famous and infamous guests throughout its nearly 122 years of service. In addition to its beautiful fountains and world-renowned hot springs, it is also rumored to be where the first teddy bear was made. For a short time the hotel turned into a Navy hospital and part of the basement was converted into a morgue. Many of the rooms have reported paranormal activity, most of which happens in the wee hours of the morning.

Before the hotel, there were the hot springs. The Ute tribe that inhabited the area knew of the waters' medicinal qualities long before any American settlers came to the area. As the settlers continued to restrict the land the Utes could live on, the hot springs were abandoned until they were discovered by Isaac Cooper, who immediately saw dollar signs. His attempts to convert the springs into a tourist getaway were largely unsuccessful. He did, however, see some improvement when his wife renamed the area Glenwood Springs instead of Defiance. The name change still did not prove to be enough, and he sold the land to Walter Devereux, who also sought to capitalize on the medicinal springs. Devereux, however, spared no expense when putting his spa together. He laid the foundations to what would be the first pool in the hot springs. After building the spa, he decided there needed to be a hotel to match.

Construction for Devereux's hotel began in 1891 and was completed two years later in May 1893. The U-shaped building had a pool in the center, complete with a fountain that shot water up to 185 feet in the air. The fountain was also electronically lit—the hotel was the first on the western slopes to have electricity. Unfortunately the fountain was covered with asphalt in 2008. In the lounge of the hotel is another pool that is filled by a 12-foot-wide waterfall. Back when the hotel first opened, the guests could sit next to this pool, which was filled with trout, and catch their own breakfast. There were 201 guest rooms available, starting at $3 a night (they now range from $110 per night to $675 per night for deluxe suites). There were also 31 ballrooms, separate entertainment areas for men and women, and 170 fireplaces. The building was modeled after the Italian Villa de Medici. Renovations and changes to hotel rooms have caused the number of guest rooms to dwindle. The hotel now uses only 130 rooms for guests. Some were converted to storage. Others, like the Presidential Suite, were converted to business centers. In its early days, the hotel operated only during the spring and summer months as it did not have a central heating system. A special railroad line was built for the hotel, attracting guests from all over the state, including Aspen, Denver, Colorado Springs, and Leadville. Of the 160 people required to run the hotel, none of them were from the Glenwood area, or even Colorado. All of the staff were brought in from Boston or England. Devereux and the others building the hotel felt it needed a certain level of class and luxury that could not be found in people from Glenwood Springs.

Shortly after the hotel opened, the "Silver Panic" hit the state. Silver was no longer being produced and was quickly dropping in value. Many of the mining settlements that had based their livelihoods on silver production were starting to fail. However, Glenwood was kept afloat by the Hotel Colorado. This is not to say that business was booming. In fact, half of the employees were given a year's salary before being politely shown the door back to Boston or England. The draw of the hot springs spa and the luxury of the hotel kept the city going.

One of the most popular famous guests was President Theodore Roosevelt. He often stayed at the Hotel Colorado on his many hunting trips to the state. The legend of the teddy bear is that on one particular trip, Roosevelt was hunting bears but was unable to bag any. The maids tried cheering him up by sewing a bear together out of scraps of fine fabric. After he did finally hunt down a bear, his daughter decided to call his trophy "Teddy." The rest, as they say, is history. There is a large balcony at the hotel that is called the President's Balcony, or sometimes the Roosevelt Balcony. Another popular guest was William "Buffalo Bill" Cody of the Wild West show. Buffalo Bill came to the springs for his health. The last known photograph of him was taken on the porch of the hotel in 1916.

While the roaring '20s were in full swing, the hotel started hosting a very different sort of clientele. Well-known gangsters such as Al Capone and "Diamond Jack" Alterie frequented the building and its gambling halls. Capone in particular spent quite a bit of time in the hotel and supposedly used one of the lift elevators to make a quick escape when authorities were searching for him. During World War II the hotel was completely converted to a military hospital and the medicinal pools were used to help ailing soldiers recover. This was when part of the hotel's basement was converted to a morgue. Dubbed the U.S. Naval Convalescent Hospital, it was commissioned in July 1943. By 1945 it had taken in more than 6,500 patients. It was decommissioned in 1946. While the hotel was serving the Navy, boilers had to be brought into the hotel as it still did not have a central heating system at the time. The Navy's presence also allowed the hotel to be modernized, and most of the electric wiring was replaced at this time. Incidentally this same idea had come up during World War I but never happened because both hotel management and the residents of Glenwood were against the idea. There is a legend of a young maid in a lover's triangle during this time. One of the men became jealous and eventually shot and killed her. The room number where this happened is not listed, but people began to claim to hear her screams from the room. Allegedly the room had so much reported activity that it became impossible to book. The hotel converted the room to storage instead.

The rest of the haunts in the hotel are not quite as violent. An apparition of a little girl with a ball is frequently seen around the hotel, as well as a Victorian woman who seems particularly fond of male guests. She is sometimes known to peer over them while they are sleeping. Other figures in period clothing have been spotted throughout the building. Sometimes a whiff of perfume is the only sign of paranormal activity. Lights have been known to turn on and off throughout the hotel, but it frequently happens in the basement, where the hospital morgue used to be. Staff members have also said that some of the doors in the area lock on their own as well. Sometimes it is the opposite problem, where doors were already locked and suddenly open on their own. Room 551 is the home of a very particular ghost. Supposedly, when the hotel was being renovated in 1982, the new wallpaper that was placed on the walls of the room bothered this ghost. Every day, staff would apply the wallpaper, only to come back and find it neatly rolled on the floor the next morning. This happened multiple times. Finally someone decided to leave samples of wallpaper on the bed. The next morning all but one had been thrown to the floor. The room was wallpapered with the selected sample, and no more problems occurred. Many people have claimed to smell cigars. Some think this may be the spirit of Devereux in the building. Many of the staff believe it could be other important figures from the hotel's past as well. The elevator has also been seen moving from floor to floor when no passengers are in it.

Room 661 is dedicated to Molly Brown, Colorado's famed resident who survived the sinking of the *Titanic*. The room is filled with memorabilia and photos of Brown. This room, and the one across (662) have both been reported to have paranormal activity in them. Of the two, Brown's room seems to be more active. Whether it is Brown specifically haunting the room remains to be seen. It is thought, however, that she haunts her old home in Denver in the Capitol Hill neighborhood. Both of these rooms are located in one of the two towers in the hotel.

Residents from Glenwood Springs, including a friend of mine who was born and raised there, think that the hotel has a creepy vibe. Some are suspicious that the hauntings may have begun once the Ute tribe was unceremoniously pushed out of the state. Others think the hotel became such a home to the people who stayed there that they simply never left its luxury.

CHAPTER 23

Hotel Jerome
ASPEN

When sumptuous Hotel Jerome opened in 1889, its amenities included electricity, steam heat, both hot and cold water, and an elevator, all luxuries that were rare at the time in Colorado.

THE SMALL CITY OF ASPEN is well known for its beauty and luxury. The ski resort brings thousands of tourists to the state in the dead of winter for snowshoeing and, of course, skiing and snowboarding. The fall and summer months are a big time for the city, as everyone migrates to see the beautiful namesake aspen trees exchange their green leaves for gold. The city's reputation has been upheld as the place to be for the nation's wealthy. Indeed, celebrities are occasionally seen staying at Hotel Jerome. Famous writer Hunter S. Thompson was sometimes seen drinking at the hotel's J-Bar. Thompson was a resident of Woody Creek near Aspen and even attempted to run for sheriff of Pitkin County. John Wayne also frequented the hotel. Celebrities of the modern era, such as Goldie Hawn and Kurt Russell, come to stay at the Hotel Jerome as well. Outside of the rare A-list sighting, guests may have a maybe-not-so-rare chance to see the spirits that reside in the hotel.

Discovery of silver brought hopeful miners to the western side of Colorado in droves. Leadville was quickly settled, and many potential prospectors did find riches. Stories of those who struck it rich only brought more men to the slopes, and soon they began to expand their search. In the hills of what is now the city of Aspen, the miners called their new settlement Ute City for the American Indian tribe that frequented the land until they were banished to present-day Utah in 1879. The name was changed to Aspen in 1880. Men were hopeful that the hills would yield bountiful silver riches, and soon those hopes were rewarded. More silver was mined out of Aspen than anywhere else in the United States. In 1879 the world's largest silver nugget was found in Aspen. It was so large it had to be cut into three pieces before being removed. It weighed a whopping 2,300 pounds. At one point miners were producing $10 million a year in the city.

Needless to say, after miners hit the silver payload, businessmen in the area hoped to make Aspen more than just a mining camp; they also hoped it would be a great city. Jerome B. Wheeler was one such man. Wheeler came from New York in 1883 and had made his fortune after becoming a partner in his wife's family firm, Macy's department store, and he wanted to bring culture to Aspen. His first step was building an opera house. The next was Hotel Jerome. In May 1889 construction on the three-story hotel began. It cost around $100,000, which was chump change when compared to the cost of some of the other hotels in Colorado. This cost included $40,000 for furnishing the building. The hotel did have electricity and, along with the Hotel Colorado in Glenwood Springs, was one of the first structures on the western slopes to have this luxury. With 90 rooms and suites to accommodate guests, it was heated with steam heat, and both hot and cold water could be found in its 15 bathrooms. The elevator was hand-operated by a rope pulley system. The opening celebration for the hotel, in November 1889, was commemorated by a grand ball.

Unfortunately, the glitz and glamour did not last. When the silver market crashed and caused several cities to lose their means of making a living, the state went into an economic depression. Aspen, like so many other cities, began to fail. Several businesses shut down, including some of Wheeler's other ventures. By some stroke of luck he was able to keep the hotel after declaring bankruptcy in 1901. During the Great Depression, the hotel continued to stay afloat by offering discounted rooms and meals. However, measures were taken to cut back on spending. The hand-pulled elevator was removed, as was the greenhouse. The bar was converted to an ice-cream parlor during Prohibition but secretly still served bourbon. Supposedly if you ordered an "Aspen Crud" you would get a milkshake with four shots of bourbon. That will keep you warm in the winter. The J-Bar now serves Aspen Cruds in homage to this legend.

It was around this time that the idea of a ski resort began forming. Skiing had been the only means of transportation for some in the winter months of Aspen, but it was quickly becoming a trendy winter sport in Europe. By 1938 some ski runs had been created, and a makeshift ski lift had even been fashioned out of abandoned mining equipment. In the '40s the hotel was modernized by its new owners and was renovated again in 1986. The second renovation temporarily knocked the number of rooms down to 23 until a fourth story with 70 rooms was added in 1988. The hotel now provides guests with the most modern luxuries, along with shuttle services to the nearby ski slopes. It is often called the crown jewel of Aspen.

Outside of its reputation for luxurious getaways, the Hotel Jerome is thought to be one of the most haunted buildings in Aspen. One of the more reported sightings in the building is that of a little boy. He is sopping wet and stands shivering in the room, wrapped in a towel. He never speaks to the guests. When people come closer to investigate, the boy disappears, leaving a wet spot or wet footprints behind. Others have urgently called the front desk to get some help for the child. When help arrives the boy is gone. Allegedly he is the spirit of a child who drowned in the hotel's pool. In 1936, as the story goes, when the boy was 10 he and his family were staying in room 310 of the hotel. He is sometimes called the "water boy" and is frequently reported as being seen by guests, most often in or near room 310.

There is apparently so much activity on the third floor that some of the staff refuse to work up there. However, Katie Kerrigan might take care of it for them anyway. Kerrigan is the ghost of a young woman who worked in the hotel as a maid in 1892, when she was 16. She was allegedly very beautiful, which did not go unnoticed by hotel guests. This made the other maids at the time jealous, and they would often play pranks on her. One of these pranks took a fatal turn when the maids told Kerrigan her kitten had escaped and fallen through the ice of a nearby pond. She went to find it, only to fall through the ice herself. She was rescued, but died of the resulting pneumonia. She has been known to do turndown service in the rooms. The larger mystery, at least to me, is what ice Kerrigan supposedly fell through. The story is she fell through the ice of a nearby pond, but I could not find one. There are no bodies of water directly by the Hotel Jerome. The closest appears to be Roaring Fork River, which is approximately four blocks away on Main Street. It could be that the pond was filled in and simply no longer exists.

Other ghostly sightings include a man who can be seen in the hallways. Sometimes there is no physical apparition of him, but guests can hear his sobs. He is thought to be Henry O'Callister, who came to Aspen hoping to find fortune in the silver mines. He was one of the lucky ones, finding a nugget estimated to be 1,500 pounds. The newly rich man also found love. O'Callister fell in love with a rich heiress from Boston and asked for her hand in marriage. Unfortunately the woman's father did not approve the match and left the man in despair—one that he apparently has yet to overcome. Lights are said to turn on and off on their own in the hotel, and some guests have noticed their heat turning on by itself as well. Travel writer Chris Gray Faust had a haunted experience in the hotel in which she and a friend found soapy water in the sink, though none of the soaps in the room had been used.

If you are a skier, go hit the slopes at Aspen. If you are not overly fond of the cold winter months, the changing of the aspen leaves is also well worth a visit. There is nothing quite like seeing a mountainside covered in gold. Take advantage of the hotel's 24-hour room service, relax a little, and enjoy your mountain stay. Just stay away from the water in the area unless you want to join Kerrigan and the water boy.

CHAPTER 24

Redstone Castle
REDSTONE

Redstone Castle, also known as Osgood Castle and Cleveholm Manor, in Redstone, Colorado, is listed on the National Register of Historic Places.

THE STORY OF REDSTONE CASTLE cannot be told without telling the story of John C. Osgood. For it is this man who built the lavish home and may still be in it to this day, haunting the mansion that survived company loss, divorce, and miner strikes.

Osgood made his fortune in the United States through the coal and steel mining industries. He came to Colorado in 1882 at the age of 31 while he was still working for the railroad. He came to the state in search of the coal reserves. The next year he

decided instead to create his own company, the Colorado Fuel
Company. Later, the company would merge with a large compet-
itor and become the Colorado Fuel and Iron Company in 1892.
When Osgood seized control of the newly formed company, it
was the largest company to produce both steel and coal in the
West. By the time 1900 came around, he was the sixth-richest
man in the country.

Osgood created a sociological branch under the Colorado
Fuel and Iron Company. Through this branch he essentially
created the town of Redstone, Colorado, which still exists today,
south of Glenwood Springs. He built more than 80 houses for
workers of the mines and their families. The houses all had
plumbing and electricity. He also built schools, an inn, and a
clubhouse in the area. The inn is still around and is currently
open as the Redstone Inn. He later acquired more companies and
expanded his land to claim more coal mines. However, Osgood
saved the crown jewel for himself. He built Redstone Castle—
sometimes called the "Ruby of the Rockies"—and made it his
home. (Redstone Castle is also the name of a house in Manitou
Springs where the Crawford family lived for a time. The two
locations are not connected, though they share the same name
and both appear to be haunted.)

Osgood's home featured 42 rooms and was a stunning
24,000 square feet. It was sometimes called the Osgood Castle,
or Cleveholm Manor, but today it is simply called the Redstone
Castle. During the time Osgood lived in the location, he referred
to it as Cleveholm Manor. It is said that Osgood spared no
expense on this lavish mansion, which was built in the Tudor
Revival style, according to the History Colorado Center. Only the
finest craftsman were brought in for the various woodworking
and other eye-catching details that would go into the finished
castle. The Redstone Castle website claims that many of the
furnishings still in the building were originally purchased by

Osgood and his second wife in antiques shops in Europe. The grand estate included servants' quarters, a gamekeeper's lodge, a carriage house, and a greenhouse. Once the building was finished, Osgood entertained important guests such as President Theodore Roosevelt, J. P. Morgan, and John D. Rockefeller. Some of these guests were often invited to the residence to participate in Osgood's hunting retreats. There is a suite named after Teddy Roosevelt in the castle. Osgood's second wife allegedly had ties to Swedish royalty and was also known to host prominent political guests from Europe. The building was completed in 1902 and cost Osgood $2.5 million, an unheard-of sum at the time. In 2015, that amount is equal to a little less than $70 million.

Osgood's success with Colorado Fuel and Iron was not to last, however. In 1903 his efforts at expansion caused the company's profits to fall short of its goals. Unable to pay debts and bills, Osgood went to Rockefeller to see if he and his family would help the company. Rockefeller and his son gave funds to the company, but only if they could seize control of it in return. Osgood left Colorado Fuel and Iron but continued to run a different fuel business, the Victor American Fuel Company. He remained a leader in the company until his death in January 1926 of abdominal cancer. This company helped keep him in the rich business circles to which he had become accustomed. Osgood is sometimes referred to as the Fuel King of the West.

In 1913, Osgood shut the estate down and left it in the care of a select few who remained in the city of Redstone. During the very early '20s, Osgood spent his time traveling throughout New York and Europe for his business. However, in 1924 he was determined to take the wheel again. He lived in Redstone Castle for the last two years of his life. His thought was to convert the castle into a resort after restoring the estate. Osgood's third wife attempted to continue his dream of making the castle a resort after his death. However, once the Great Depression hit, it became clear that this would not happen. Much of Osgood's estate, including Redstone Castle, was sold. By 1941, part of Osgood's legacy, the town of Redstone, Colorado, had a population of just 14 people.

In the 1950s and '60s there were attempts at making the city of Redstone a ski resort. A lift was built, and one of the few remaining smaller buildings of Osgood's estate was converted to a ski lodge. However, due to the city's proximity to Aspen, Colorado, the attempts were unsuccessful. Over time and a few attempts at renovations, the Redstone Castle became a historical landmark in 1971, albeit an endangered one. Many of the homes built for miners in the early 1900s were sold to new residents. During the '90s the castle was run as a bed-and-breakfast. Later, a man who purchased the house at an auction was indicted by the IRS for criminal fraud. In 2003 the IRS seized the castle, claiming it had been purchased with profits from fraud. It was the first home ever sold via online auction to pay off the victims of the owner's schemes. The auction opened in March 2005. Some residents were concerned that the new buyer would plan to demolish the castle, a fear that would never have been realized due to the castle's status as a historic landmark. The winning bidder paid $4 million for the house. The new owner reopened the building for tours in 2007. It was also this owner who began the major restoration process of the home. According to the city of Redstone's website, the entire exterior was completely renovated in 2010. Currently, the castle is not open as a resort as the restoration process has not been completed, but visitors can access the building for tours. Tours take place daily in the summer and on weekends in the winter.

In a *Denver Post* article from 2005, a business columnist jokingly warned that whoever purchased the Redstone Castle would not be living there alone. The article mainly refers to the theory that Osgood is still in the building. The writer also jokes that the ghost of the owner who committed fraud could be there as well begging for money. (The owner's partying lifestyle caused him to die of a heart attack before being put to trial.) Osgood seems to be a more likely candidate, although the smell of phantom cigar smoke could be attributed to the ghost of the other owner as well, as he was known to be a heavy partier. Cigar smoke was reportedly smelled near the closed door of what used to be Osgood's bedroom. No one else was in the castle at the time. The columnist spoke with the curator of Redstone Castle, who at the time had lived in the castle for the last six years. One of the reports the curator made was of spirits that would hover in the secret passageway (a requirement for all large castlelike homes, apparently) that connected the nursery to the servants' quarters. Some say that Osgood's second wife, Lady Bountiful, as some of Redstone's early residents used to call her, is sometimes known to make appearances as well. It is said that you can smell her perfume or the fragrance of fresh lilacs in what used to be her quarters. At one point when the house was on the market in the '80s, psychics were brought into the building. Allegedly they did not find much but sensed a presence in the Teddy Roosevelt Suite.

Despite the massive size of the castle, this particular story of the Fuel King of the West, John C. Osgood, is just a small facet of the man's life. But the home held such great importance to him and his second wife that they still visit now and then, even though it has been nearly 90 years since Osgood's death. But with a home like that in the beautiful Rocky Mountain countryside, who would ever want to leave?

CHAPTER 25

Gilpin County
CENTRAL CITY AND BLACK HAWK

A view of the splendor of the Central City Opera House from the stage. Actors such as Mike Dougherty, who is one of the alleged spirits in the building, saw this view every night they performed.

GILPIN CASINO

THE CITY OF BLACK HAWK, COLORADO, is one of the state's own gambling getaways. Many of Colorado's gambling locations, Black Hawk included, are small towns that look like they have barely moved since the times of the Old West. Many of the buildings have the same look and feel as they did back then. However, they do have one notable exception: the flashing lights of hundreds of slot machines.

Black Hawk, like so many other cities in the Centennial State, was a gold mining city. The first time gold was discovered in the area was in 1859, when it was still considered part of the Kansas Territory. The settlement formed by thousands of would-be miners who came to the state for the Pikes Peak gold rush was called Mountain City. As the city population dwindled to the more serious miners, it took on a new name: Black Hawk. Many attribute this to the American Indian chief. It would become one of Colorado's first cities, incorporated into the territory on March 11, 1864, and would be connected to Denver by train in 1872. Gold mining was the main occupation in the city, which was at one point called the "richest square mile on Earth." The city would later face a long, slow decline after the silver crash in the late 1800s. The gold mines slowly emptied. It was not until 1991 that the idea to allow limited-stakes gambling in the state was formed. Two casinos were opened and, according to the city of Black Hawk's website, these casinos helped the city bring in revenue of $20,000 daily.

The Gilpin Hotel Casino opened in 1992 in the original Gilpin Hotel building. At some point, the building stopped running as a hotel, though many websites still list it as the Gilpin Hotel Casino. Currently, it is strictly a gambling hall and casino. There is also, however, a restaurant in the casino. It is called Lucille Malone's, named for a ghostly legend surrounding the building.

Although information on the original building is harder to find, it is said that it was built in 1869 and was strictly a hotel and bar back in the city's mining days. Upstairs, there was a one-room school for the small town. The teacher, Lucille Malone, is the alleged source of the building's hauntings. Malone was in love with a miner, but tragedy struck when this miner was run over by a wagon and killed. Malone would later throw herself over the hotel balcony. Some versions of the story say that the miner was not just Malone's lover but also her fiancé.

Reports from Malone's are of people seeing a woman walking around the building, but upon closer inspection, she is gone. She is sometimes described as wearing a white blouse with a black skirt. She was seen near the area that used to be the dining room when the building still functioned as a hotel. During this time, the hotel owners could rarely keep the room filled that supposedly housed Malone's ghost. She was known to throw suitcases and bags on top of the guests staying in the room. Some have reported lights turning on by themselves. According to a *Denver Post* article from 1996, during construction to make the building into a casino, several construction employees said windows would blow open by themselves, no matter what they did to close them.

CENTRAL CITY

CENTRAL CITY, COLORADO, is maybe a stone's throw away from Black Hawk. Their proximity meant that both cities were popular destinations for the miners and prospectors coming to the Centennial State. The two cities were even settled around similar times, as the year people began settling in Central City was also 1859. However, Central City was incorporated two years after Black Hawk, in 1886. Many of the mines that brought people to the city have been covered with concrete slabs in more recent years. This is to protect people from falling in, as it is estimated that some of the deeper ones go down as far as 2,000 feet.

While Central City followed the path of Black Hawk into the gambling business, it is also home to one of the nation's oldest cultural organizations as well: the Central City Opera. The opera group is the fifth-oldest in the country, in company with the

Many of the buildings in mountain towns look much the same as they did when they were first built. The Gilpin Casino in Black Hawk used to be a hotel but has now joined the ranks of casinos in the city. The building is supposedly haunted by Lucille Malone, who has a restaurant in the building named in her honor.

Metropolitan Opera in New York and the San Francisco Opera in California. Central City's Opera House was built in 1878, though it would not be home to the opera group until its formation in 1932. Residents wanted the opera house built so that the city would begin to match the reputation it had acquired due to its wealth of gold.

Like so many things in Colorado, when the mines began to dry up, so did the Central City Opera House. It was in disrepair until citizens volunteered to restore it in 1932. The grand reopening was celebrated with the opera *Camille*, which brought forth the tradition of the summer opera festival that continues today. It was also the birth of what would become the Central City Opera company. Fun fact about the opera house: when new

seating was added in 1999 it was decided that the faces of notable Coloradans would be carved on the backs. Pioneer Buffalo
Bill is one of those who can be found looking back at you as you
enjoy a performance at the opera house.

For readers who have not worked in theater, a little-known
fact about the glamorous people who sing and dance onstage
is that they are, stereotypically at least, a fairly superstitious lot.
There is a long-standing tradition that when the stage is not
being used, stage hands leave what is known as a ghost light on
the stage. It is usually a simple light on a pole, put directly in the
middle. It is meant to keep the theater's ghosts away. While I am
unsure if the Central City Opera follows this superstition, there
are a few ghosts that possibly haunt the building.

Back when the theater was first being built, there was supposedly a miner who turned to acting once the opera house was
built. His name was Mike Dougherty. According to the story, he
was quite a favorite in the town. However, Dougherty fell prey to
alcoholism and supposedly drank himself to death. But his love
of the stage carries on, as does, unfortunately, his love for booze.
Visitors standing in the backstage area have said they have gotten
a whiff of strong alcohol. In some instances the smell is followed
by a pat on the shoulder or something playing with people's hair.
The entity is, of course, unseen during these pranks. Orbs have
also sometimes been seen moving into the wings on the dark
stage. The ghost of a female patron is thought to occupy the
balcony where she used to sit and enjoy performances. It is said
you can sometimes hear her footsteps as she moves across the
area. Maybe the small-town theater does not need a ghost light,
as it seems that both their ghosts are fond lovers of the arts.

Additional Haunted Sites

Near the heart of downtown Denver, and just a hop, skip, and a jump away from the capitol, is the central branch of the Denver Public Library. The building's warm light and welcoming atmosphere make it hard to believe that it could be haunted, but allegedly a cranky ghost lives in the basement. *(See page 179)*

Additional Haunted Sites

Capitol Hill Thug

Denver Public Library
(Central Branch)

Lumber Baron Inn and Gardens

Macky Auditorium at the
University of Colorado Boulder

Gold Camp Road

College Inn at the University
of Colorado Boulder

Meeker Massacre

Old Chapel
McIntyre House

CHAPTER 26

Capitol Hill Thug

DENVER

THE CAPITOL HILL THUG, also known as the Capitol Hill Slugger, was a man known for a series of attacks and eventually murders of women in the early 1900s. Women of varying ages were attacked in the Capitol Hill area. The attacks were characterized by lone women walking in the street being attacked from behind and hit over the head with what Denver police and *The Denver Post* thought could be anything from a lead pipe to a sandbag. Usually the women were hit once in the back of the head, with a few exceptions. None of them were sexually assaulted, and very few were robbed, making police question what the motive of the attacker was. Many of the victims claimed that their attacker had the unusual floral scent of violets. This was a clue the police thought would lead to an arrest. In the end, it never gave them any answers. Today, however, it may provide a warning to women walking the streets of Denver that his ghost is near.

The attacks began in June 1900 and continued until January 1902. Three of the women attacked died from their injuries. The three fatal attacks were Lillian Bell, Josephine Unternahrer, and Mary Short. Both Short and Unternahrer were attacked on the night of February 22, as was a third woman by the name of Emma Johnson. On February 25, 1901, only a day after *The Denver Post* wrote an article offering a $100 reward to anyone who had either information or was able to give up the thug "dead or alive," a man named Albert Cowan was arrested. He was arrested only as a "suspicious character" and was one of many men arrested on suspicion of being the thug.

All police accounts of Cowan presented him as a mentally unbalanced man who did not seem to trust anyone. However, this did not hold much stock with the public because all of the men arrested were claimed to be insane in some way by the police. Another thing that did not hold was Cowan's physical description. One victim, Emma Carlson, was able to give a description of her attacker, and neither Cowan's appearance nor his clothing was a match. One report in a newspaper claimed that a witness saw the attacker wearing what looked like a police uniform. However, witnesses against Cowan began to come forward, including a man named W. H. Lowe, who sent a letter to the police. Lowe wrote that while living in Las Vegas, Cowan was known as Bug House Davis. Lowe also claimed that Cowan would often rave that the world would be better off without women and in a few years they would be killed off. However, Cowan told police that he had never been anywhere near Las Vegas and did not know who Lowe was. Cowan's trial began on March 26, 1901. Witness Albert Frederick was on hand to testify that he had caught Cowan in the act. Frederick's story was that a woman passed him as he was crossing a vacant lot. After she had passed him, he heard her scream and turned to see a man hovering over her with his arm lifted holding something shining in his hand. Frederick claimed that he moved on from the woman as he did not want to become involved in the fight. Shortly after, a man he identified as Cowan passed by him.

Frederick's story would be cross-examined by Cowan's defense and was later dismissed. It came out that Frederick was a morphine addict, and people suspected that he chose to come forward as a "witness" only to claim the reward, which had gone up to $900 by then. Additionally Cowan had several witnesses of his own who provided his alibi as well as testimony against the city's charges of insanity. Cowan was eventually released and charges were dropped. After his arrest, the thug, who had lain low during the trial, attacked again. This time when police came to arrest him, Cowan was found in his apartment sound asleep. Cowan eventually left the city of Denver, and while the attacks continued for a short while, they eventually stopped. The Capitol Hill Thug was never brought to justice.

There are theories that the Capitol Hill Thug still roams the streets today. Kevin Pharris, haunted-tour guide and author of *The Haunted Heart of Denver,* said in his book that he frequently would bring his tours through areas where some of these attacks occurred. On three occasions people walked through something similar to a cold spot, but instead of cold air it was a strong floral smell. This by itself could be nothing, but Pharris believed it to be the ghost of the thug because, in addition to the scent, the women in his group began to feel very uncomfortable as well.

CHAPTER 27

Denver Public Library (Central Branch)
DENVER

THE EVERYDAY PERSON WHO WALKS INTO the central branch of the Denver library system may see little to suspect they have entered a haunted place. The large building has more of a modern architectural style with several different-colored brick sections outside, while the inside has large windows on each floor letting in lots of sunlight. The small tables that allow readers to sit and enjoy their finds give the building a homey feel. I have never felt a cold presence or any cold spots in the library. In fact, the only negative feeling I have ever sensed was my own anxiety over finding the right sources for college papers in years past. Despite the cheer of the upper floors, a ghost may reside in the basement of the building.

Denver Public Library has held a place in the city for 125 years. Librarian John Cotton Dana opened the first public library in a wing of Denver High School. The first stand-alone library building was completed and located near Civic Center Park downtown in 1910. Between 1913 and 1920, eight other libraries were planned. Both projects were funded with the help of Andrew Carnegie.

The original location continued to be used until 1956, when the current location opened at Broadway and 14th Avenue. It was more than twice the size of the original, but due to population booms in the city, it was expected to meet Denver's needs only for the next 10 years. Four more libraries were added to the system during this time.

However, in the late 1980s Denver libraries were facing a problem. Their collections were becoming too large for the library buildings to handle. In addition the libraries were not compatible with advancing technologies. The central branch in particular had a collection so large that only one-quarter of it was on display in the building; the rest was stored. In 1990, 75% of voters approved a bond issue of $91.6 million to renovate and expand the central branch as well as the other 12 branches. Both projects were completed in 1995, and a new 540,000-square-foot central branch was opened.

Currently, the children's section holds 15,000 items in the basement. According to a blog on the library's website, the reason some books are stored is because they are fragile, rare, or no longer in print. However, the same blog mentions the possibility of the library being haunted by an old librarian. There is not much information on the ghost outside of that. People are unsure of his name, or whether it is indeed the ghost of a librarian. However, it is supposedly a less-than-pleasant spirit and has been known to shove people. Reportedly, it also made several night guards quit, which caused a change in security: the guards patrol in pairs now.

CHAPTER 28

Lumber Baron Inn and Gardens
DENVER

The Lumber Baron Inn and Gardens in Denver is supposedly haunted by two young women who were murdered there; their cases were never solved.

ONE HOTEL IN THE DENVER AREA that does not shy away from its haunted past is the Lumber Baron Inn and Gardens, also known as the Lumber Baron Mystery Mansion. Like many hotels, the Lumber Baron provides guests with a comfortable place to stay as well as a venue for weddings and other events. What the hotel also has is a whole collection of mystery dinners. Tickets for the annual mystery dinner season can be found on their website.

The real lumber baron was John Mouat, a Scottish immigrant who built the mansion after acquiring his fortune in the lumber industry in the 1890s. Mouat's company built more than 200 buildings in Denver. His own house, built for himself, his wife, and their five children, included many different types of wood, including cherry, oak, and walnut. When completed, the house was 8,500 square feet. After the Mouats, the house was passed to different families before being converted into separate apartments. This is where the horrors of the so-called mystery mansion come in.

By 1970 the mansion had been converted into individual apartments. One 17-year-old from Golden, Colorado, named Cara Lee Knoche, had started living in the building in September of that year. She had previously dropped out of high school. On Oct. 12, 1970, both Knoche and Marianne Weaver, a high school friend of hers, were found dead in Knoche's apartment. Knoche had been raped and then strangled to death. She was found naked and shoved under the bed with a knife underneath her. There were signs that she struggled with her attacker and tried to protect herself. Weaver, on the other hand, was found lying on top of the bed with a shot to the head. The police suspect she may have walked in on the murder, in turn to be murdered herself. She allegedly left her parents' home in Lakewood around 9 p.m. to visit Knoche. Unlike her friend, Weaver was not sexually assaulted. The women were discovered by a friend of Weaver's who saw her car outside the building. It was around 3 a.m. on the 13th, and the friend thought it was odd that their lights were off, as the girls were known to party, and went to check on them. According to an article in *The Denver Post* published the day after the murders, the lock appeared to have been jammed. Because Knoche and her roommate had reported a break-in prior to the attack, the broken lock was no surprise. The thief had stolen $280 worth of their belongings. Knoche's roommate was in California at the time of the murders. During the investigation, other residents told police that people had tried to visit Knoche that night but were surprised to find her door locked. When questioned, the building's landlord stated that the women often had many male guests in the apartment and frequently had parties. Knoche's father told *The Denver Post* in October 2014 that he thought the murder was drug related (police did find a small bag of marijuana in the apartment). He also said the murder came the day after Knoche had turned 17 and told her parents she would be moving out of the apartment later that week. She had also expressed a desire to return to school. In 2014, 44 years after the death of the two girls, police still are no closer to finding the murderer, and the case is one of Denver's many cold cases. According to Phil Goodstein's book *The Lumber Baron Inn: Denver's Mystery Mansion,* the lead detective on the case would call the inn from time to time before his death to share memories of the case in the hopes that it would eventually be cracked.

The two girls are often thought of as the cause of any paranormal activity that happens in the building. Apparitions of young women have been seen, and the sound of footsteps has been heard. In one case the image of Weaver was thought to be seen in the reflection of a mirror photographed at the inn. In the Valentine Suite, which is where the girls were murdered, some guests have said that they felt something hovering near them. Both images and recordings of cats have been made in the Valentine Suite, even though there was no cat on the premises at the time. Some psychics who have investigated the building claim to have contacted the two women. While they did

supposedly go into detail about their deaths, there was unfortunately no information about the killer.

On the other hand, some of the paranormal activity is unre-
lated to Knoche and Weaver. Some claim that Mouat may still
haunt the building. Cold spots have been felt throughout the
building as well and the house creaks and groans despite heavy
renovation. There is also the figure of a woman in Victorian
clothing that can be seen on the stairwell. Some also claim it
is her shadow you see in the mirror above the fireplace in the
front parlor. Some people have also claimed to see a tall woman
in a blue dress from the '20s. Additionally they can smell the
cigarette smoke she leaves behind, despite a no-smoking policy
in the building. The owner claimed a teenage ghost would greet
him in the basement every day as well.

After the murders in the '70s, the building began to crumble. The next owners, Julie and Walter Keller, found the building
in the '90s and decided to restore it. Their job was not an easy
one, as the building was so dilapidated it had been condemned
by the city, but it is now considered one of the best examples of
original Queen Anne architecture in Denver. The Kellers did not
shy away from the paranormal aspect of their hotel and hosted
paranormal investigations there on many occasions. But despite
booming business, they placed the Mystery Mansion back on
the market in June 2014. It sold in April 2016 for $1.7 million
to Elaine and Joel Bryant, who will continue to operate it as a
bed-and-breakfast.

Macky Auditorium at the University of Colorado Boulder

BOULDER

The University of Colorado Boulder is the largest university in the state. The tragic tale of a young woman's murder in the auditorium has become the stuff of legend on campus.

MANY OF THE SITES IN COLORADO have earned their haunted reputation due to a gruesome act that happened in the location or building. Unfortunately the Macky Auditorium on the campus of the University of Colorado Boulder is no exception. In July 1966 a young student named Elaura Jeanne Jaquette was brutally raped and murdered in the building. Since

her death, students have reported numerous stories of paranormal activity there, specifically in the room where she was
killed. University officials, on the other hand, claim that it is a
way for students to make light of a horrible situation that happened on campus and insist the building is not being haunted
by her ghost.

Macky Auditorium is named for Andrew J. Macky, a resident of the city of Boulder who gave the university $300,000 in
his will after his death in 1907. It was considered the second-
largest gift to be made to the university at the time. Groundbreak-
ing for the building began in 1909 and was completed in 1922.
The university itself, which opened in 1877, is considered one of
the most beautiful in the United States. Naturally, the Macky
Auditorium followed suit. It holds a pipe organ that cost the university $90,000, only $20,000 of which came from the Macky
estate. The remaining amount was raised by the school. It is one
of the more well-known buildings on campus and has hosted
concerts by some famous performers over the years as well as
some of the university commencement ceremonies. The very
first concert was held in the building on May 19, 1923.

On the day of her murder, Jaquette, a zoology student at
the university, was sitting outside having lunch in the grass
near the Macky building. She was waiting for the children she
babysat to finish a movie in a nearby theater. She would never
see the kids again. Her wallet and remaining lunch were found
alone. Later that afternoon, her body would also be found in the
organ room in the west tower of the building. She had been raped
and brutally beaten.

Thirty days after the slaying of Jaquette, a man named
Joseph Dyre Morse was arrested. He was a janitor for the university, age 37. His two teenage daughters claimed to have
seen him carrying a bucket of bloody clothing on the day of
the murder. His fingerprints were also a match for one found

at the crime scene. Prior incidents of unwanted sexual advances and violence by Morse were dug up, and it was determined that his violence came out most when he was drinking. Morse had been seen drinking earlier in the day of Jaquette's murder. He was sentenced to 888 years in prison, although he did not officially confess to the murder until 1980. Morse never told anyone how he convinced Jaquette to follow him up to the organ room. Friends and family say that she sang and had a love for music and suspect that Morse may have taken advantage of that interest. Some websites on paranormal locations wrongly report that Jaquette was already in the room practicing on the organ. Morse later died in prison at the age of 77 in 2005.

Since Jaquette's death, people have claimed to hear unexplained footsteps as well as the organ playing on its own in the west tower area. Some people have heard talking or singing throughout the building and have seen apparitions of a woman or a man in a brown suit in the auditorium. The most horrifying account of paranormal activity is people claiming to see blood splattered on the walls. The haunts allegedly began five years after Jaquette's death. The area is now the office of a retired professor. Unfortunately so many students have tried to get into the area for dares to determine how haunted it really is that this professor has had to block the area off. Indeed, when the Rocky Mountain Paranormal Research Society investigated the building, they caught students breaking in with sleeping bags. These break-ins happen more frequently around Halloween.

During their investigation of the building in 2009, Rocky Mountain Paranormal Research Society could not find anything out of the ordinary, and no unexplainable events occurred during their occupation of the building. However, they said that is not necessarily conclusive proof that the building is not haunted. They have not posted any additional investigations of the Macky on their website. Remaining members of the Jaquette family insist that, due to her very spiritual nature, Elaura would not wish to remain behind to haunt this world; she would rather be with God. It seems that the story of her murder has transcended into its own reality for students at the University of Colorado Boulder.

CHAPTER 30

Gold Camp Road
COLORADO SPRINGS

COLORADO SPRINGS LIES IN THE HEART of the Rocky Mountains, and it is naturally one of the best places in the state for hiking due to its location. The gold rush that brought many of the pioneers and potential miners to the area was sparked in part because of the mountain that rises high above the city and its neighbor, Manitou Springs. "Pikes Peak or bust" became a legend in and of itself.

Once people began flocking into the area, so did the railroads. One of these railways was called the Short Line. It was a quick ride from Colorado Springs southwest to Cripple Creek, another mining town. After the invention of the automobile, this railway area was converted into a toll road in the '20s and eventually into a free public road after that. Gold Camp Road includes hiking trail that follows the path of the old railway. There were originally nine numbered tunnels that ran through the mountains. One of the tunnels, number 3, has since collapsed and is fenced off. Since the tunnel's collapse, the city has created detours to keep cars on track. It is an 8.6-mile trip on the dirt trail for hikers, but drivers must be prepared to go about 43 miles to get to Cripple Creek. Instead of being able to cut across using the Gold Camp Road to go west, drivers have to go north to get to a highway that will take them back southwest toward Cripple Creek. By day the area is quite beautiful and has breathtaking views. While various trail websites and hikers will tell you that it is a medium-level or moderate hike, many others will tell you not to bother going to the area. It is known to be an area where bodies of crime victims have been found in the muddy sides of the road. At least three murders have occurred in the area within the last 10 years. One of the victims was a 19-year-old woman who was allegedly raped before being killed. It is also a popular area for alleged satanic worship and ghosts.

Gold Camp Road has amassed a reputation over the years. Many of the residents will argue over the cause of tunnel 3's collapse. The reasonable explanation is rotting timbers in the '80s and fires later in the mid-2000s. The most popular story, however, and the source of many of the alleged haunts in the area is that a school bus driver either had an ill-timed heart attack or committed suicide by driving into the side of the tunnel in a blaze of fire in 1987. No one, including the school-age children on the bus, survived the crash. Some insist that no school would have used buses to travel through this tunnel as it is too narrow. Others say that it is a fabricated story used to keep children and teenagers out of the area. If that is the case, then the stories have changed with the generations, as others argue that the ghostly activity is due to a train conductor who was decapitated upon entering the tunnel. Although the tunnel is fenced off, people have been able to walk up to the entrance, and some have even braved the inside. Those who have traveled inside the tunnel claim to see blood spots on the ceiling and walls. However, in October 2011, a paranormal hunter told the *Pikes Peak Courier* that the blood spots people claim to see are actually rust and that there is no evidence of a bus crash. There have been reports of a little girl saying "hey" and the sounds of children laughing. Some say you can hear the schoolchildren laughing and giggling in tunnels 1 and 2, but you hear their screams in tunnel 3.

Despite arguments about the cause of ghostly activity, there is agreement on the creepy feel and even some of the ghostly activities in the tunnels. Many teenagers and young adults in Colorado Springs go into the other tunnels as sort of a dare.

Some park their cars in the middle of the second tunnel, where more violent activity is reported. People have reported everything from scratches and voices to being hit and sometimes even groped by unseen figures. Some suspect that pokes and scratches come from the phantom children killed in tunnel 3. The wildest reports even include stories of possession. There are also stories of activity dealing with the cars themselves. Some cars won't restart, lights won't work, or the radio has strange issues. People also claim that they have found handprints on their cars after leaving. Most often, these reports come in conjunction with sightings of a man pacing at the end of the tunnel or leaning on its rocky walls. Others claim that any and all "ghostly" activity is caused by teenagers trying to scare people. There is a large amount of debate as to the legitimacy of the ghosts in Gold Camp Road, but it is undeniably an urban legend of which every resident of the city is aware.

CHAPTER 31

College Inn at the University of Colorado Boulder

BOULDER

IN 1999, students living at the College Inn at the University of Colorado Boulder experienced a very strange phenomenon. People had claimed the building was haunted for quite some time with several accounts of strange sounds, misty specters, voices, elevators moving on their own, and footsteps. Most of this activity seemed to be happening on the third floor. The building had no record of murder or suicide that the owners knew about, but that did not stop some people from claiming to see ghostly blood splattered on the walls. The incident from 1999 however, was different. Each room had an old-fashioned globe-style lamp. In some accounts of the story, the lamps were nailed down to prevent theft. These nails did not stop every lamp in every room from falling to the floor at the same time one night.

Constructed in the 1960s, the building was used as a dorm until the 2010–2011 academic year. After that it was used as an overflow location for student housing. It could also be used as a conference space. In 2008 it was determined by the school's annual safety inspections that the building had a serious asbestos problem. Students had to sign notifications and safety precautions before moving in. In 2013 the university demolished the College Inn, as renovating the building and removing the asbestos would cost the school more than the building was worth. At the time of demolition, there was no plan for what would go in the space instead. The lot was simply covered with gravel. Now that there is no building to investigate, the reasoning behind the strange occurrences may never come to light.

CHAPTER 32

Meeker Massacre
MEEKER

WHEN SETTLERS FIRST MOVED TO COLORADO
they found it occupied by American Indians. The Homestead
Act drove more people toward the western mountainous area
of Colorado. The rumors of gold were a draw as well. This land
was originally the home of the Ute tribe, who called the land
the Shining Mountains. Unfortunately, throughout the years
of settling Colorado, and many of the other states in the Wild
West, people continually shoved the native tribes into smaller
and smaller land areas. Some of the leaders, like Chief Ouray
(meaning Arrow) of the Ute tribe, were peaceful. Ouray in particular would frequently give passing settlers advice on the area.
It was he who advised Alferd Packer's group of hopeful prospectors where to go before the large storm that brought them to
their unfortunate fate (see page 134). A city in Colorado is now
named in Ouray's honor. Others of the tribe were not as peaceful. Violence broke out, and both settlers and Indians were killed.
This violence did nothing to help the cause, but only fanned the
flame. The death of a white family led directly to the atrocities
of the Sand Creek Massacre (see page 94). Tensions between
the two were only increasing. White settlers started protesting,
and newspapers in the north were blazoned with the headline
"The Utes Must Go!"

When the whites first came to settle in the western slopes,
the Utes were not unfriendly. But the continued shrinking of
their lands created adversity. In 1868 the Utes had signed a
treaty with the Americans that restricted their lands. The plots
they were "given" were considered to be ancestral, so this deal
was at first agreeable. Next they signed a treaty that was to create

boundaries on the land, but the Utes agreed before the limit of their land was decided. Later they found out their best land was going to be taken from them. Ouray began to lose control of his lesser chiefs, who began pillaging in the area. The job of maintaining relations in the White River area with the Ute tribe was hard to keep filled. The position had already turned over to a few people before Nathan C. Meeker took over.

Before taking the post, Meeker had been sent to the slopes by his employer, *New York Tribune* Editor Horace Greeley. Meeker and 50 other families founded the city of Greeley, Colorado, in 1869. He applied to become the agent at White River eight years later. Meeker had met with few successful endeavors in his life, and unfortunately his post at White River was not one of them. Appointed in March 1878, he was 60 years old when he took the job. His plan was to try and make the Indians less nomadic and more like the American farmer. Unfortunately, this good-intentioned misunderstanding of the culture helped lead to his death. Meeker enforced many changes on the White River Ute, such as religion and living in houses instead of tepees. Meeker was stricter with food rations than previous agents had been. The tribe also did not like the miners that were now coming to the city in droves. For them to remove the precious gold ore from the bowels of the mountains was an offense to their gods. The straw that broke the camel's back, though, was taking the land the Utes used for pony racing and converting it to farmland. This caused the Utes to become restless. Until then, Meeker had been resistant to bringing troops into the area, knowing it would only anger the Utes more. He finally caved in and called in troops in September 1879.

Unfortunately, Meeker had been right to think that bringing in the military would anger the tribe. One of the chiefs, Chief Johnson, injured Meeker after seeing the military's approach. Later the tribes were found performing an all-night war dance despite instructions not to do so. On the morning of September 29, the head chief of the area, Chief Douglas, was having breakfast with the Meeker family. They all seemed in good spirits and Meeker was healing fine from his previous injuries. Despite how well the meal seemed to be going, Douglas left abruptly after another tribesman came to speak with him. It is now believed that the other man was there to warn Douglas that the attack on Meeker was set. Shortly after Douglas left, the Utes came up to the Meeker house and began firing their weapons. Ten of Meeker's male employees were killed without much hope of fighting back. Meeker's wife, his daughter Josephine, and a friend with her two children were in the other room doing dishes. Upon hearing the gunfire they all fled to the milk house. The Indians smoked them out of the building and then took them prisoner. Meeker's wife was allowed to go in the house to retrieve her Spirit Book. It was then that she saw the body of her husband, who had been shot to death. Later it would be discovered that his body was mutilated by the tribes after his wife left. Meeker's wife was shot in the hip during the fight and remained crippled for the rest of her life.

The women and two children were held captive by the Utes for more than three weeks, causing the American public to stew over the latest Indian attack. Ouray rode to find the traveling Utes that held the Meeker women captive. It is largely due to his efforts that they were released. Both Josephine and Mrs. Meeker would later say they believed that the Ute leaders from White River thought Meeker was damaging their reputation via the newspaper and that he was at fault for the anti-Ute headlines. Unfortunately for the tribe, the attack would be one of the final nails in their coffin. The attack became known as the Meeker Massacre (or the White River Massacre to some). Following the massacre, there was another attack on the military by the Utes called the Battle of Milk Creek. Six months after the massacre and following attack at Milk Creek, Congress ordered that all Utes be removed to reservations in Utah. It was called the Ute Removal Act. The town of Meeker was founded in 1883 in the White River area. It was named in honor of Nathan Meeker.

Meeker's ghost is said to haunt the small area of land where the massacre occurred, some 90 miles from the city. Those who have seen it say that it is a gruesome sight to behold. Although Meeker died from a mere gunshot wound, his mutilated body was later found among the burning buildings his family had resided in when he was acting as agent. His ghost takes on the destroyed form of his corpse. The arms appear to have been hacked off, and the form is covered in gashes. It is said his mouth is open in a permanent scream. Outside of this horrific description there is not much information about this haunted site. The location of the massacre is marked simply, off the side of the highway, with a large wooden sign.

CHAPTER 33

Old Chapel

LAMAR

OUTSIDE OF DENVER AND THE FRONT RANGE, Colorado is a little bit more of a rural state. The cities are further spread out across the plains in the east and the mountains in the west. Despite some of the horrific histories behind the various ghost stories in this book, murder is also not very common in the state—especially in the more rural cities, such as Lamar.

The city was founded in December 1886. In 2010 the census reported a little under 8,000 people living there. It is certainly the type of city where most everyone knows each other. Knowing this small-town dynamic makes it all the more shocking to hear about the haunting at the Old Chapel.

Due to the horror of the story, finding any historical information on the actual site is difficult. Most sources immediately tell of the murder of a priest and nun and the rape of a second nun. The ghost stories build on the second nun discovering she was pregnant and later hanging herself from a room in the infamous chapel. People have said she can be heard crying and moaning in the building, and some reports have seen an apparition of her as well.

Unfortunately, this smells to me of another urban legend gone horribly wrong. While it is sometimes difficult to find historical information on a location, it is unusual to find absolutely none. After doing a generic search for "The Old Chapel" I found information on the alleged haunting, but not on the building itself. A search for murders in Lamar came up empty as well. I decided to narrow my search even further by looking up murdered priests in Lamar. I still turned up zilch. The only information that ever pops up on the location is the story of the double homicide of the priest and nun, and the eventual suicide of a second nun. None of the sources include names or even a location of the chapel. With such an interesting, albeit horrible background story, I was hoping this location would yield more information. It goes to show that in the age of the Internet we can have all the answers in the palm of our hands and still have no answers at the same time. With ghosts and ghosthunting being so wildly popular, it is becoming less and less surprising to see ghost stories popping up online. However, not finding any information on the location outside of the alleged haunting was a red flag for me in doing research.

CHAPTER 34

Colorado Springs Pioneers Museum
COLORADO SPRINGS

Located off South Tejon Street and East Vermijo Avenue, the Pioneers Museum in Colorado Springs used to be an old courthouse. A custodian, shot by another employee, supposedly haunts it.

FOR COLORADO, THE DAYS OF THE PIONEERS are a strong part of its cultural heritage. The city of Colorado Springs decided to renovate the El Paso County Courthouse into a museum dedicated to that very heritage: the

Colorado Springs Pioneers Museum. The location also happens to be haunted, but not by pioneers or Western historical figures; it is haunted by someone of a more recent past. Supposedly the museum is haunted by an old manager who was murdered by a disgruntled employee.

The El Paso County Courthouse was first built in 1903. From that time until 1973, the building functioned as the headquarters for Colorado Springs' administration and government, as well as the local court. It was restored to its former glory and transitioned into the Colorado Springs Pioneers Museum in 1979. The building is on the National Register of Historic Places. The predominant feature is a large domed clock tower. Admission is free, and the building is located in one of the parks in downtown Colorado Springs, making it a family-friendly experience.

The Pioneers Museum focuses largely on the history of the Pikes Peak region. Its permanent collection features more than 60,000 items, which include pottery; regional art; and items from the Ute, Arapahoe, and Cheyenne tribes. In addition to the permanent exhibits, it also has temporary exhibits, a schedule of which can be found on the website. The museum kept the old courtroom, which is not only used as an exhibition but can also be used for weddings. Perhaps one of the most important parts of the museum is the Starsmore Center for Local History. This library, like the museum, concentrates on the Pikes Peak region and contains early photographs of Colorado Springs, newspaper collections, as well as city directories dating back to the 1870s. The center also has the personal papers of the city's founder, Gen. William Jackson Palmer.

The story behind the alleged haunts of the building is this: a manager of one of the government agencies in the building was murdered in his office by an employee who became enraged after he thought he had been cheated out of part of his paycheck. This is how you see the story told on several websites when doing research on the subject. However, *The Gazette*, a local Colorado Springs newspaper, went a little deeper in an October 2007 story called "Residual Residents." According to the story, the victim, Eddie Roy Beals, was a custodian for the courthouse. Some accounts list him as the chief custodian. He was shot five times by fellow custodian Willie Butler on May 29, 1959. There is a grave with Beals's name and date of death in the Evergreen Cemetery in Colorado Springs (this cemetery is also supposedly haunted but not by Beals). There are also articles from the early 1960s about the trial after the murder from the *Colorado Springs Gazette Telegraph*. The Internet does seem to have one thing right: the dispute was about money. Supposedly, one of Beals's favorite hangouts is the elevator. The elevator door must be opened by hand, but this does not seem to stop it from opening on its own when there is no one inside it. Allegedly Beals was shot in front of the elevator, which may explain his fixation on the location.

CHAPTER 35

McIntyre House
Douglas County

WHEN LOOKING AT GHOST STORIES and haunted locations, you often come across accounts of people at their darkest. It is a history of people showing what truly horrible things humans are capable of when pushed to the far reaches of a need for something. The story of the McIntyre House is one such story.

In southeastern Colorado there is a place near Coyote Gulch where it is said you can hear a man screaming for his life during strong thunderstorms. At first glance it may just seem like another Internet horror story: a wealthy traveler coming from Denver during the times of the Old West was brutally murdered on his way to Pueblo. More digging however, yields more information.

The McIntyres were just another average pioneer family who settled into what is now Douglas County. Their community was called Coyote Gulch, and the residents there quickly learned to stay away from them. The father was a nasty and unpleasant man, and the reputations of his two sons, Jack and Jim, were even more dubious than their father's. With no aspirations or skills to speak of, the McIntyre sons turned to their neighbors for income—by stealing from them. The boys also rustled cattle. Needless to say, the surrounding people knew that the McIntyres were trouble and left them alone.

When a group traveling by stagecoach from Denver to Pueblo came through Coyote Gulch in 1875 (another version of the story places it in June 1871), a man was accidentally left behind at the 20 Mile Stop. The traveler decided to attempt to walk to the next stop, which was 10 miles away in a settlement called Russellville.

But a heavy thunderstorm broke out, causing the man to look for shelter. Unfortunately for him, he found it at the McIntyre house. It is unclear which of the McIntyre men birthed the plan to murder this man in his sleep, but that is exactly what followed after they fed the traveler dinner and lent him a spare room for the night. It is said that the man was in an upstairs room and that the boys climbed through the window to get into the room. The first attempt at stabbing the man in the chest did not kill him. He awoke screaming in agony. This led to a struggle, but the McIntyres won in the end. The man was a wealthy banker, and the McIntyres stole his money, gold watch, clothes, and boots. Their good fortune would not last long, however.

There are two versions of how the story ends. One version is that people began to search for the traveler when he did not appear in Pueblo. The search party somehow made their way to the McIntyre house, finding blood all over the upstairs bedroom. The other version is that a group found the body of the traveler and immediately suspected the McIntyres. In both versions of the story, the boys confess to the crime and say that their father had nothing to do with the murder. However, only Jim would hang for the crime. Jack was able to slip away in the chaos. The McIntyres were never seen in Colorado again.

To me, it is understandable that the traveler's spirit may remain in the McIntyre House. To die in such a brutal fashion, while thinking you are safe in someone else's home, may cause you to have a little hate for the world. Several years later a couple was traveling to Franktown when they became stranded by a thunderstorm. They also sought shelter at the McIntyre house, without realizing its history at first. Sometime during the night the couple heard a blood-curdling scream from somewhere in the house. The man ran upstairs and thought he saw someone go out the window. The wife at this point had realized which house they were in. Upon deciding it was the traveler's ghost they were hearing, the couple decided that braving the storm did not sound so bad anymore. It is said that the scream could be heard in the Coyote Gulch area for another 10 years.

On face value, this story appears to be yet another exaggerated tale of grisly life in the Wild West. A general search for the McIntyre house will give you a page that describes the details of the murder. A more specific search on the hanging of Jim McIntyre directs you to a page stating that a Douglas Channel news station (DC8TV) aired a Halloween special on the McIntyre murder. The special can be seen on the station's YouTube channel under Legends and Oddities. However, there is another website that lists every Colorado execution that happened legally here. There is no Jim McIntyre in any of the 102 records listed. However, that could also mean that a mob hanged him, and not the state. Additionally, it is unclear where the McIntyre house is in Douglas County. While the city of Franktown still exists, Coyote Gulch is no longer the name of the area. Franktown lies slightly southeast of Denver, 91 miles away from Pueblo. It is also unclear whether or not the house still exists, and if it does, it could be privately owned. It seems to be yet another location with a great background story but not enough information.

Colorado Haunted Road Trip Travel Guide

AMERICA'S

HAUNTED ROAD TRIP

Visiting Haunted Sites

COLORADO IS A FAIRLY EASY STATE to understand
geographically. Its rectangular shape is split, very nearly in the
middle, by the Rocky Mountains. Chapters in this book are orga-
nized into five areas: Denver, just north of the middle, and (clock-
wise around the state) the Front Range, East, South Central, and
West. We advise that ghosthunters know all they can about sites
before visiting them. Updates to this section can be found on the
Ghosthunting Colorado blog (ghosthunting-colorado.blogspot.com).

DENVER AREA

ESTABLISHED AS a mining town, Denver is the capital of
the state and the seat of Denver County. The city is home to
more than 600,000 people, and some 3.2 million populate the
Denver-Metro Area. While Denver is not in the mountains, it is
very close to them, and 200 named peaks can be seen from the
city. Boasting 300 days of sunshine a year, it is nicknamed the
Mile High City because it sits at an elevation of 5,280 feet. Sites
described in this book that are in Denver are divided between
the locations in the Capitol Hill neighborhood (Patterson Inn,
Cheesman Park and the Denver Botanic Gardens, and the Molly
Brown House Museum) and those in the rest of the city.

CAPITOL HILL
Patterson Inn 303-955-5142
420 E. 11th Ave., Denver, CO 80203
pattersoninn.com

THIS MASSIVE RED SANDSTONE MANSION, completed in 1891, had mystery surrounding it from the beginning. For most of its existence, it was privately owned and
used and a personal home by its various owners throughout the years. At one point,
it was used as an office building. However, it was purchased and then renovated by
architect Brian Higgins, who now runs it as an inn with themed rooms.

Cheesman Park
Franklin Street and Eighth Avenue, Denver, CO 80206
HOURS ARE from 5 a.m. (for brave-at-heart early-morning joggers) to 11 p.m. The park stretches right up to the property line of the Denver Botanic Gardens.

Denver Botanic Gardens 720-865-3401
1007 York St., Denver, CO 80206
botanicgardens.org
THE GARDENS ARE OPEN daily, 9 a.m.–5 p.m. Tickets can be purchased directly through the website or on site. During the summer they frequently have special exhibitions as well as a concert series. On winter nights they have Blossoms of Light, in which many of the gardens' trees and bushes are hung with lights.

Molly Brown House Museum 303-832-4092
1340 Pennsylvania St., Denver, CO 80203
mollybrown.org
FROM JUNE THROUGH AUGUST, the museum's hours are Monday–Friday, 10 a.m.–4:30 p.m.; Saturday, 10 a.m.–4 p.m.; and Sunday, 12–4 p.m. All other times of the year, the hours are Tuesday–Saturday, 10 a.m.–4 p.m., and Sundays, 12–4 p.m. (closed on Mondays). Tour tickets are sold at the museum in the carriage house visitor center on a first-come, first-serve basis. They start every half hour. The only way to see the inside of the house is through a tour.

DENVER
Oxford Hotel 303-628-5400
1600 17th St., Denver, CO 80202
theoxfordhotel.com
OPENED IN 1891, the Oxford is Denver's oldest hotel. The building was one of the first in Denver to have elevators, or vertical railways, as they were called at that time. The bar in the Cruise Room was the first bar to open in the city after Prohibition.

American Museum of Western Art 303-293-2000
1727 Tremont Place, Denver, CO 80202
anschutzcollection.org/museum/navarre-building
THE AMERICAN MUSEUM OF WESTERN ART is located across the street from the Brown Palace Hotel. It is included in the "Denver's Infamous Brothels" chapter (page 42) as it used to be home to the Navarre brothel. The museum is a part

of the Anschutz Collection and is open for tours only on Mondays and Wednesdays. Guided tours take place at 10 a.m. and 1 p.m., but the museum is also open for self-guided tours from 10 a.m. to 4:30 p.m.

Mattie's House of Mirrors
1946 Market St., Denver, CO 80202

THIS IS THE ORIGINAL LOCATION of Denver's more legendary brothel: Mattie's House of Mirrors. At one point the spot housed a bar named after the brothel, but now it is owned by Lodo's Bar and Grill, which has a great rooftop view of Coors Field (the Colorado Rockies' baseball stadium) but bears little resemblance to the original location, as all the mirrors have been removed. There is a plaque commemorating the spot, however, in front of the building.

The Brown Palace Hotel 303-297-3111
321 17th St., Denver, CO 80202
brownpalace.com

THE BROWN PALACE COMPETES with the Oxford as the second-oldest hotel in Denver. It opened a year after the Oxford in 1892, but the Brown Palace argues that it has been open the longest, as it has never closed its doors since it opened. The Oxford, on the other hand, spent a brief time closed while it was being renovated.

Tivoli Student Union
900 Auraria Parkway, Denver, CO 80204

The Tivoli Student Union is the student recreational center on the Auraria Campus in downtown Denver. The building is home to a pool hall, lounges, the bookstore, and several campus offices. While much of this building is reserved for students, there are several places where you can get food inside. The lower level is done in more food-court style, but you can also find spaces to order a meal and sit down. The building was originally used as a brewery, and the campus recently started producing beer there again.

FRONT RANGE

DENVER AND THE FRONT RANGE make up the most populous region of Colorado. There are several cities in the area, but the most well known is Boulder, seat of Boulder County and home to the main branch of the University of Colorado. One of the United States' most haunted buildings is in the Front Range: the Stanley Hotel. Another city in the Front Range, Fort Collins, is home to Colorado State University, the second-largest school in the state.

Buffalo Bill Museum and Grave 303-526-0744
987½ Lookout Mountain Road, Golden, CO 80401
buffalobill.org

GOLDEN IS THE FIRST TASTE of the mountains as the West moves from the flatter plains into the foothills. The Buffalo Bill Museum has great views of the area as it is perched on one of these hills. You can see the grave for free, but the museum has a small ticket fee. In the summer the museum is open daily, 9 a.m.–5 p.m. Winter hours are the same, but Tuesday–Sunday only. Golden is also one of the best places in Colorado to go river tubing. There is only a small window of time in the summer when water levels permit, but it is a fun way to lean back, enjoy the view (maybe some snacks), and float down Clear Creek. For more information on rentals, water safety, and other tips, go to tinyurl.com /cowatersport.

Red Rocks Amphitheatre 720-865-2494
18300 W. Alameda Parkway, Morrison, CO 80465
redrocksonline.com

RED ROCKS AMPHITHEATRE is a great spot to visit, no matter the occasion. There are hikes around the stage area, and people also use the steep stairs to exercise. Fewer options are available during the winter, but during the summer there are concerts and movies. A full schedule of activities can be found on the website. On event days the amphitheatre closes at 2 p.m.

Hotel Boulderado 303-442-4344
2115 13th St., Boulder, CO 80302
boulderado.com

BOULDER IS FARTHER INTO the mountainous areas of Colorado. This sizable college town is home to a little more than 100,000 people. The Hotel Boulderado was first opened on New Year's Day in 1909. The city wanted to be considered a more cultural city and decided a hotel was necessary to do that. The name, voted on by the citizens, combines city and state and was chosen so that people would always have a way of remembering where they stayed. The hotel is located right next to the Pearl Street Mall, an outdoor mall that stretches four blocks in the heart of the city. The mall has a combination of local and national chains, as well as stores unique to Boulder. A full list can be found at boulderdowntown.com/shopping. Other tabs on this site will take you to dining options and the history of the Pearl Street Mall. There are also numerous opportunities for hiking and other outdoor activities in Boulder.

Boulder Theater 303-786-7030
2032 14th St., Boulder, CO 80302
THIS THEATER IS BLOCKS AWAY from the Hotel Boulderado. The restaurant attached to the theater used to be named for the ghost that supposedly haunts the building but is now simply called the Ghost and sells barbecue. The theater is open for tickets sales Monday–Saturday, 12–6 p.m. In addition to concerts, the venue also screens films. A list of events can be found on the website. The Ghost is also open Monday–Saturday, 11 a.m.–2 p.m. and 4–10 p.m.

Stanley Hotel 970-577-4000
333 E. Wonderview Ave., Estes Park, CO 80517
stanleyhotel.com
THE STANLEY HOTEL IS SUPPOSEDLY the most haunted location in the state and arguably the country. It is, at the very least, a well-known location. Part of this is due to Stephen King's novel *The Shining*. King and his wife were the only guests in the hotel at the end of the season one year, and the rest, as they say, is history. The hotel by itself has a lot to offer guests, including tours and dining. It is also right next to Rocky Mountain National Park, which is accessible year-round—Trail Ridge Road is great for scenic driving. Be sure to check the weather. In Colorado, mountain driving can become very dangerous, and some roads will start to close due to weather. The park is also the natural habitat for more than 1,000 elk. The best time to see these animals is in the fall.

EAST

THE ROCKY MOUNTAINS divide the state of Colorado almost cleanly through the middle. What many people forget is that the eastern part of the state is mostly flat; the northeastern area is known as the Great Plains. This half of the state is one of the most sparsely populated areas in all of the United States. Towns are usually small, and some of them are built around farming communities.

Similarly, the southeastern portion of the state is not heavily populated. The large stretches of plains look almost exactly as they did when they were being settled in the mid-1800s. The area is home to hundreds of different kinds of birds, including bald eagles. Portions of the east are sad reminders of the battles between the American Indians living in the area and the Americans trying to settle there.

SUMMIT SPRINGS BATTLEFIELD

Some of the land on which the battle occurred is on public property. However, some of the roads through the area are blocked off with signs that say NO TRESPASSING, and due to an unfortunate amount of vandalism, the landowners have restricted public use even further. They have been known to allow some people access after speaking with them. Both of the monuments, and additional markers, are accessible to the public. Directions are out of Sterling, Colorado, which is almost due north of Otis, where the battlefield is located. Take I-76 south 10 miles, exiting at Atwood. Continue south on CO 63 for around 5 miles to County Road 43. There will be a sign for the Summit Springs Battlefield. At the sign, head east for about 2 miles. Otis is about a two-hour drive from Denver. It is close to Morgan County, which has a little more information for tourists: morgancountytourism.com.

Sand Creek Massacre National Historic Site 719-438-5916
55411 County Road W, Chivington, CO 81036
nps.gov/sand/index.htm

IN 2000, Colorado Senator Ben Nighthorse Campbell sponsored a law to make the site of the Sand Creek Massacre a National Historic Site. President Bill Clinton would later sign that law, officially giving the National Park Service permission to acquire 7,680 acres of land. This section of land is found 40 miles north of Lamar, Colorado, and is open for visitors daily April 1–December 1, 9 a.m–4 p.m. From December to March the hours are the same, but the park is closed on weekends. Chivington is about a 3-hour drive from Denver, or a 2½-hour drive from Colorado Springs.

South Central

MOVING BACK TOWARD THE WEST, visitors enter South Central Colorado. The second-largest city in the state, Colorado Springs, is a popular destination. It is the seat of El Paso County and has a population of close to 440,000. The most well-known mountain in the area is Pikes Peak, views of which can be seen throughout Colorado Springs and its neighbor Manitou Springs. Manitou is a much smaller city, with a population of a little more than 5,000. Manitou also has the reputation of being more of a "hippie" city. It even has a citywide motto: "Keep Manitou weird."

Broadmoor 719-634-7711
1 Lake Ave., Colorado Springs, CO 80906
broadmoor.com

THE BROADMOOR is the crown jewel of Colorado Springs. It is consistently ranked as one of the top hotels in the state and is rated as a AAA Five-Diamond and a *Forbes Travel Guide* Five-Star hotel. The hotel is in the Cheyenne Mountain area, home to the Cheyenne Mountain Zoo. Spencer Penrose, original owner of the Broadmoor, had a collection of exotic animals that was used to create the zoo. His shrine looms above the city near the top of the peak, a strange reminder of his presence. The Garden of the Gods area, also near the Broadmoor, is full of hiking trails and large red sandstone formations.

Cave of the Winds 719-685-5444
100 Cave of the Winds Road, Manitou Springs, CO 80829
caveofthewinds.com

CAVE OF THE WINDS is millions of years old. Numerous types of cave life, such as bats and insects, can be found in the caverns here. In addition to cave tours, the area also has amusement park rides and games. The whole area near Manitou and the Springs is filled with various hiking trails. However, some were closed after the Waldo Canyon fire in 2012. Be sure to check out any information on trails online in advance. A map of the caves, which outlines the routes of the different tours available, can be found on the Cave of the Winds website.

Miramont Castle 719-685-1011
9 Capitol Hill Ave., Manitou Springs, CO 80829
miramontcastle.org
ALL TOURS AT MIRAMONT CASTLE are self-guided. The summer season runs
Memorial Day–Labor Day, when it is open daily, 9 a.m.–5 p.m. During the
winter the museum is open Tuesday–Sunday, 10 a.m.–4 p.m. The Tea Room hosts
special events throughout the year or can be booked for private events. The castle
also has a garden that is open in the spring and summer.

Museum of Colorado Prisons 719-269-3015
201 First St., Cañon City, CO 81212
prisonmuseum.org
THE POPULATION OF CAÑON CITY is approximately three times larger than that
of Manitou. The museum offers firsthand views of what life behind bars can be
like. It also has information on and historical items that belonged to infamous
inmates. One such inmate is Alferd Packer, the first person in the United States
to be tried and jailed for cannibalism. It is also close to the Royal Gorge Bridge,
which has breathtaking views of the surrounding areas.

WEST

FEW PLACES REMIND YOU of the Old West like Colorado.
The city of Durango is where many Wild West–themed movies
were filmed. Southern Colorado is also home to two features
unique to our state: the Four Corners and the Mesa Verde cliff
dwellings. The Four Corners Monument is the only location
in the United States where you can stand in four states at once
(Colorado, New Mexico, Arizona, and Utah). The Mesa Verde
area was inhabited by the Ancestral Puebloans, who eventually
moved their dwellings right into the side of Mesa Verde. However, they abandoned their cliffside home by 1300.

Coming full circle to the northwestern area of Colorado
means entering ski country. The majority of Colorado's 25 ski
resorts are scattered throughout this area. While traveling
through Colorado it is important to remember a couple of things:
First, Coloradans love their weekend getaways to the mountains,

no matter what time of year it is. This means that traffic in and out of the mountains can be heavy. Travel times could easily double or even triple. The second is that Colorado weather is unpredictable. There is running joke that if you do not like the weather, wait five minutes. As a native Coloradan who has spent 20 years in the state, I have never heard a joke that rings more true. Several years' worth of getting snowstorms in May (in Denver) will teach that to you. This means that it is important to check the weather and road conditions, particularly when traveling in the mountains. The main highway going west is I-70, and Eisenhower Tunnel is the main route to almost all of Colorado's ski country. If the tunnel has been closed due to weather, it is almost a guarantee that road conditions are not safe.

Durango & Silverton Narrow Gauge Railroad 970-247-2733
479 Main Ave., Durango, CO 81301
durangotrain.com

THE DURANGO & SILVERTON Narrow Gauge Railroad guides you down the original tracks used to transport goods between the two towns. Each end has a museum. The route is through the mountains and provides spectacular views of the area. The organization also has guided tours of mines in Silverton, as well as a guide of the Mesa Verde cave dwellings.

Rochester Hotel 970-385-1920
726 E. Second Ave., Durango, CO 81301
rochesterhotel.com

WHILE RENOVATING the hotel, the current owners decided to keep some of the Rochester's Old West charm by keeping several antique items from the hotel and some of its original woodwork. Each room is themed as a Wild West movie that was filmed in the Durango area.

The Historic Brown Hotel & Restaurant 970-453-0084
208 N. Ridge St., Breckenridge, CO 80424
historicbrown.com

BRECKENRIDGE IS PART OF a cluster of small mountain towns near the end of the Eisenhower Tunnel going westbound. Not to be confused with the Brown Palace in Denver, the Historic Brown was also built in the late 1800s. Their bar and restaurant is open daily, 7 p.m.–2 a.m. One thing to remember with ski resort towns is that summer is their slow season. Some locations shut down or have restricted business hours in summer.

Country Boy Mine 970-453-4405
0542 French Gulch Road, Breckenridge, CO 80424
countryboymine.com

SOME LOCATIONS, like the Country Boy Mine, have better hours in the summer. The mine is open daily, 9:30 a.m.–5:15 p.m., during the summer season. Tours of the mines start on the hour, beginning at 10 a.m. and ending at 4 p.m. During the fall it is open only on weekdays, 10:30 a.m.–2:15 p.m.; tours are still on the hour but begin at 11 a.m. and end at 1 p.m. The mine is closed during the winter and spring.

Après Handcrafted Libations 970-423-6700
130 S. Main St., Breckenridge, CO 80424
apreslibations.com

THIS LOCATION has changed hands and names several times, but the haunted legends remain the same. Après Handcrafted Libations is a drinks-only joint open daily, 2 p.m.–12 a.m.(ish), according to its website.

Hotel Colorado 970-945-6511
526 Pine St., Glenwood Springs, CO 81601
hotelcolorado.com

GLENWOOD SPRINGS has several hot springs throughout the city. Locals and tourists alike go there for romantic, or just relaxing, getaways. There is also great camping in the area.

Redstone Castle 970-963-9656
58 Redstone Blvd., Carbondale, CO 81623
redstonecastle.us

BECAUSE REDSTONE CASTLE IS under the long process of being renovated to become a resort and spa, the only way to see the building is by guided tour. During the summer there are daily tours starting at 1:30. The gates of the castle will open at 1:10. During the other seasons they recommend you check the online calendar to ensure that a tour is happening on the day of your choice. In summer it is OK to buy tickets the day of, but they recommend booking in advance for other seasons because space is limited.

Hotel Jerome 855-331-7233

330 E. Main St., Aspen, CO 81611

hoteljerome.aubergeresorts.com

ASPEN IS ONE OF COLORADO'S more luxurious ski resort cities. It also has some cultural institutions, such as the Wheeler Opera House, which is named for the same man who built Hotel Jerome (Jerome Wheeler). Locals have a favorite time of year to visit Aspen and the surrounding area: fall. Every year, usually around the end of September, the aspen leaves begin to change from green to a beautiful golden color. Seeing the mountainsides covered in vast stretches of gold is really quite breathtaking.

Gilpin Casino 303-582-1133

111 Main St., Black Hawk, CO 80422

thegilpincasino.com

THIS SMALL CASINO CITY is about an hour and a half south of Estes Park. As with all mountain cities, it is close to several hiking trails. For the nongamblers, there is also dining in the city.

Central City Opera House 303-292-6700

124 Eureka St., Central City, CO 80427

centralcityopera.org

CENTRAL CITY OPERA HOUSE is home to the fifth-longest-running opera company in the country. They have a short window where they perform in their own opera house before packing up and touring throughout the rest of the state. More information on the season can be found on their website.

Ghostly Resources

FOLLOWING ARE SELECT RESOURCES affiliated with this book that road-trippers and paranormal researchers can use to more fully explore haunted sites in Colorado and learn more about ghosthunting in general.

Many purportedly haunted sites also have excellent websites devoted to them and their non-haunted histories, and we have listed a number of these in the sections on Visiting Haunted Sites. Additionally, many cities have their own websites with complete tourist information, which could include ghost tours as well as other non-paranormal activities. Be sure to also see the Bibliography (page 218) for potentially useful sources of information that do not appear here or in the other sections.

Ghosthunting Colorado (blog) ghosthunting-colorado.blogspot.com
This is the official blog for *Ghosthunting Colorado*. It is a multimedia site that contains material based on author Kailyn Lamb's personal visits to haunted places throughout the region as well as possible special events.

Kailyn Lamb (Facebook page) facebook.com/kailyn.lamb.7
This is Kailyn Lamb's official page on Facebook and one of the main venues she uses for posting information about recent pieces she has written. Follow it to get exclusive information not available anywhere else. She can also be found on Twitter under the username @kailyn_l.

America's Haunted Road Trip (website) americashauntedroadtrip.com
This is the official website of the America's Haunted Road Trip series of travel guides to haunted places people can visit and, among other things, features articles on haunted sites throughout the country.

America's Haunted Road Trip (Facebook page)
facebook.com/AHRT.books
This is the official Facebook page for the America's Haunted Road Trip series of travel guides and a source for information about this book and others in the line, author events, and more.

Bibliography

FOLLOWING IS A LIST of sources used in the research for *Ghosthunting Colorado*. For the most part, this section does not include websites that are listed elsewhere in this book, such as the sections on Additional Haunted Sites and Ghostly Resources.

Baker, Dennis. *Ghosts of Colorado*. Atglen, PA: Schiffer, 2008.

Bueler, Gladys R. *Colorado's Colorful Characters*. Chicago: Johnson, 1975.

Goodstein, Phil H. *The Ghosts of Denver: Capitol Hill*. Denver: New Social, 1996.

Goodstein, Phil H., and Walter Keller. *The Lumber Baron Inn: Denver's Mystery Mansion*. Denver: New Social, 2013.

Hafnor, John. *Strange but True, Colorado: Weird Tales of the Wild West*. Fort Collins, CO: Lone Pine Productions, 2005.

Leggett, Ann Alexander, and Jordan Alexander Leggett. *A Haunted History of Denver's Croke-Patterson Mansion*. Charleston, SC: History Press, 2011.

Lyons, Sandy Arno. *Colorado's Most Haunted: A Ghostly Guide to the Rocky Mountain State*. N.p.: SkateRight, 2011.

Murphy, Jan Elizabeth. *Mysteries and Legends of Colorado: True Stories of the Unsolved and Unexplained*. Guilford, CT: TwoDot, 2007.

Newman, Rich. *The Ghost Hunter's Field Guide: Over 1000 Haunted Places You Can Experience*. Woodbury, MN: Llewellyn, 2011.

———. *Ghost Hunting for Beginners: Everything You Need to Know to Get Started*. Woodbury, MN: Llewellyn, 2011.

Perry, Phyllis J. *Speaking Ill of the Dead Jerks in Colorado History*. Guilford, CT: Globe Pequot, 2011.

Pharris, Kevin. *The Haunted Heart of Denver*. Charleston, SC: History Press, 2011.

Stansfield, Charles A. *Haunted Colorado: Ghosts and Strange Phenomena of the Centennial State*. Mechanicsburg, PA: Stackpole, 2011.

Waters, Stephanie. *Haunted Manitou Springs*. (Haunted America, 2011).

WEBSITES

Boulder Country Paranormal Research Society
coloradoparanormal.tripod.com/index.html

Breckenridge Heritage Alliance breckheritage.com

Colorado Springs Ghost Hunters csghosthunters.com/20901.html

Denver History Tours denverhistorytours.com

Denver Post **Blogs** blogs.denverpost.com

Frontrange Paranormal Investigations parafpi.com/main.html

Ghost in My Suitcase ghostinmysuitcase.com/places/miramont

Ghost Towns ghosttowns.com/states/co/summitspringsbattlefield.html

Haunted Colorado hauntedcolorado.net

Haunted Places hauntedplaces.org

Haunted Places To Go haunted-places-to-go.com/brown-palace.html

Haunted Rooms hauntedrooms.com

Legends of America legendsofamerica.com

National Park Service nps.gov

Paranormal Stories Colorado paranormalstoriescolorado.com

Rocky Mountain Paranormal Research Society
rockymountainparanormal.com

Stanley Film Fest stanleyfilmfest.com/about

About the Author

KAILYN LAMB is a journalist who received her bachelor's degree in multimedia journalism from the Metropolitan State University of Denver and her master's degree from Columbia University's Graduate School of Journalism in May 2016. She is a Colorado native and has written for Denver's own *Out Front* magazine. *Ghosthunting Colorado* is her first book. She currently lives in New York City. She has an online presence through social media sites, primarily Facebook and Twitter.